Blog: http://jamesgemitchellblog.wordpress.com

Email: jamesgemitchell@gmail.com

Instagram: jamesgemitchell

Twitter: @jamesgemitchell

Written by James G.E. Mitchell and published on December, 31 2020

CONTEMPORARY COLONIALISM THROGH MULTICULTURALISM

Chapter 1:
Canada the white country of immigrants.

> *It was the initial European immigration that began the destruction of the Indigenous people and their lands so how can importing even more non-Indigenous people through multiculturalism make things better?*

The very common saying that "Canada is a country of immigrants" is all-to-often cited by politicians and open border advocates as a means to justify large scale immigration programs and to silence any critics of multiculturalism. Canadians are regularly reminded that the success of the country was formed on the basis of immigration and that it was immigrants who built the economic foundation and who made sacrifices for everyone, past and present.[1] These sacrifices are proclaimed to be the reason why Canadians have it so good today in terms of an excellent economy, individual liberties, universal health care, public education, a social welfare system and many other public programs that ensure a way of life that far exceeds what other countries provide for their citizens. That's what makes Canada so attractive to many people around the world who are impoverished due to circumstances beyond their control and who are seeking a better way of life. The idea that Canada offers people a better life is the reason why immigration has been steadily and rapidly increasing thereby reinforcing the concept that Canada is a country of immigrants that was built by immigration. These initial immigrants were the product of a colonial establishment that wanted to populate the nation

---

[1] https://www.canada.ca/en/immigration-refugees-citizenship/corporate/publications-manuals/annual-report-parliament-immigration-2018/report.html

with its own people and the people that would benefit the colonial cause: the colonial cause of occupying and using the land of the Indigenous people. The initial immigrants who settled on the Indigenous people's land in Canada were clearly not Indigenous themselves; they were a product of the colonial powers who had a goal of pillaging the lands and resources in order to build a nation that was reflective of what European colonialism represents. There's no doubt that Canada is a country of immigrants in terms of how it was settled by European colonists and how the concept of immigration has been consistently increasing over the last century. Just because Canada has been consistent on its immigration intake over the last century doesn't necessarily mean that there's an obligation to maintain such consistent numbers. Maintaining a consistent intake of non-Indigenous people – under the concept that Canada was built on immigration – is a complete injustice to Indigenous people and their future success. It was the initial European immigration that began the destruction of the Indigenous people and their lands so how can importing even more non-Indigenous people through multiculturalism make things better?

This is certainly a perplexing question because it highlights a major contradiction between the harmful effects of colonialism and the mass immigration of early Europeans, while at the same time, crediting the concept of early immigration as the *foundation* to a successful contemporary society. This *foundation* is what is argued by many people as the reason why large scale immigration must continue and why immigration must be recognized as a key component to Canada's national identity and history. This is how and why the rhetorical concept stating that immigrants built the nation from the ground up – so that life today is bountiful in so many ways – begins to manifest itself as a justification for continued immigration thus leading to the overuse of the term describing Canada as a nation of immigrants. It is further surmised that we must therefore open our doors to more immigration as a token of understanding and appreciation for the national privileges that we possess. The irony begins to reveal itself when simple consideration is given to the analysis between the professed damage colonial immigration has done to Indigenous people and their lands and how it was immigration that has made, and continues to make, Canada a great nation. This concept of believing that immigration is necessary, solely because the country was founded and built by immigrants, is only a concept that a white person could think of and has become an all too common theme in contemporary Canadian society. Initial European colonialism had a major focus on bringing white people to Canada as early settlers to build the social, cultural and economic foundation of the country in order to reflect the colonial establishment of white Europeans. The colonial establishment is one that was aimed at implementing whiteness as a social standard and it used immigration as a means to do so by importing massive amounts of non-Indigenous people into Canada.

• • • • • • • • • • • • • • •

Author and anti-racist activist Tim Wise has lectured at hundreds of colleges across the United States and has written books that are mandatory reading for graduate level social science and humanities courses in Canada. Wise is a committed advocate of immigration into the United States and he also believes strongly that the entire structure of the U.S. is overrun with *whiteness*. This *whiteness* is what Wise believes is one if the root causes of racism in the U.S. and many other white majority countries including Canada. I was first exposed to Tim Wise and his writings when I was a graduate student, focusing on equity studies, when I read his book entitled White Like Me: Reflections on Race From a Privileged Son. Wise reflected on many personal anecdotes that detailed his racial experiences in the U.S. and how these experiences demonstrates the oppression of non-whites by the white majority. Wise also stresses how there is an inherent aspect of white privilege occupying the social structure of many communities and how this white privilege results in covertly expressed racism. Citing how the police are more likely to pullover, stop and frisk or arbitrarily question a non-white person as opposed to someone white, Wise makes a well-intended case that colonial based societies are racist by default and that whites are beneficiaries of their white skin colour thereby resulting in covert racism. It is for this reason that the police are less likely to bother whites, whites are more likely to get better jobs, whites are more likely to get a better public education, whites are more likely to have better housing and are more likely to have greater personal wealth. Wise has also chimed in on how the white structure in America has decimated the American Indigenous people by displacing them from their lands and forcing them to be subjected to white laws and oppression. Tim Wise even acknowledges that his own ancestors were complicit in the appropriation of Indigenous lands that subjected Indigenous people to white oppression.[2] Nevertheless, Wise is revered as a spokesperson for the racial underdog and is rarely refuted in his opinions and anecdotes regarding racial inequality. The paradoxical element of Tim Wise is that he highlights the racial inequality of colonial based societies – such as Canada – and how this inequality is a direct result of European colonial policies that allowed large scale immigration of non-Indigenous people into Indigenous lands, while at the same time, he advocates open borders and large scale immigration into the very same lands that once belonged to the Indigenous people. Large scale immigration

---

[2] http://theweeklychallenger.com/by-the-color-of-their-skin-tim-wise-on-the-myth-of-a-postracial-america/

seems to be perfectly acceptable and reasonable so long as it doesn't reflect the original European colonial model of immigration that endorsed a European culture of whiteness. The breakdown begins to occur when open border advocates overlook how the entire concept of immigration into a white settler country is something that is premised on the importation of non-Indigenous people into indigenous lands. Overlooking how immigration today is different than it was in the colonial era is a simple as applying semantics and renaming immigration to multiculturalism. This is how open border advocates like Tim Wise can justify their demands for large scale immigration as an achievement of racial equality while criticizing past colonial immigration as being a form of white oppression.

Colonialism: What is it?

> *Even though vast areas of North America were not necessarily occupied by Indigenous people, there is still the modern day conception that the land had, and still does, belong to the Indigenous people of today.*

Colonialism is the *dirty* word that critical race theorist use regularly to describe how white oppression victimized the Indigenous people of a colonized land. According to Noam Chomsky, colonialism is a powerful system subduing others usually for some kind of *resources*.[3] *Resources* refers to a nation's land and environmental materials such as oil, gas, gold, silver, spices, animals or crops of many sorts. In Canada, initial European occupation had a focus on the fur trade, which was very valuable to the white occupiers. The Indigenous people used fur, but only to the extend that they needed it and they certainly didn't profit from it. The concept of profit during the early European occupation of North America was a major driving force that pushed the white man further into Indigenous lands. Even though vast areas of North America were not necessarily occupied by Indigenous people, there is still the modern day conception that the land had, and still does, belong to the Indigenous people of today. This is where the contentious issues of Indigenous rights begin.

Nomadic Indigenous peoples in North America may not have had specific title to the land they used but they did have a spiritual connection to it. The resources that the Plains people relied on were buffalo, bison, deer, elk and many more animals that provided food, clothing and fuel making it necessary to follow the resources

---

[3] https://settlercolonialstudies.blog/2014/04/04/noam-chomsky-on-settler-colonialism/

wherever they roamed.[4] The concept of material possession and ownership of land to the Plains people was not what it was to the European occupiers. Robin Ridington draws this comparison between nomadic hunting and gathering people who had no need for the European technology and its concept of *ownership*. Ridington suggests that the idea of owning irrelevant material things would have been a burden due to the fact that the Indigenous hunters and gatherers had to move and follow the resources. Instead of trying to control nature with technology, as the European occupiers did, the Indigenous people focused on controlling their relationship with nature.[5] The argument from a Eurocentric standpoint is that the Indigenous people never really owned the land to begin with but merely used parcels of it for their way of life. From the standpoint of the Indigenous Plains people, the land belonged to them spiritually as it gave them what they needed to maintain their way of life and any interference with that was a great violation of their natural and spiritual connection to the land. Their territory/area/land therefore had no borders, boundaries except for what nature established.

This raises the most important question regarding Indigenous sovereignty and how it can be defined by land ownership: who owns the land? Although Canadian law acknowledges that Indigenous people may hold an ongoing title to their lands that predate European occupation, the courts have never definitively affirmed such a title. There has been a number of landmark court cases over the years that have set standards for Indigenous land use based on historical connections, but no actual rights of ownership that would be title worthy. In the 2013 Supreme Court of Canada case of William v. British Columbia, the courts ruled that indeed Indigenous title to the land included a beneficial interest whereas the Crown retained underlining control of such land. This is inline with the early landmark SCC case of R v. Sparrow where it was ruled that Indigenous rights such as fishing, hunting and gathering were protected under the Constitution and couldn't be infringed upon without justification due to the Crown's fiduciary duty to the Indigenous people.

These two cases essentially established that the use of land has a historical connection to the Indigenous people and can't be infringed upon unless the government undertakes prudent consultation with them. These two landmark cases also infer that there is no legitimate or specific title available to Indigenous people that would allow them to establish any form of self-government resembling a republic. Instead, Canada's Indigenous people are a protected product of the

---

[4] https://www.thecanadianencyclopedia.ca/en/article/aboriginal-people-plains

[5] Ridington, Robin. "Technology, World View, and Adaptive Strategy in North American Hunting Society." *Canadian Review of Sociology and Anthropology* 19, no.4 (1984): 469-480

Crown and then assigned, or allowed to use, occupy and or inhabit specific areas away from European style settlements.[6] Today a vast majority of Indigenous reserves are in areas outside of the mainstream cities and the members who live on them don't own title to their property. Indigenous reserves in Canada are regulated by the federal government under the Indian Act and are communities with exclusive membership usually based on family kinship.[7] This essentially means that the European common law system doesn't recognize any formal connection to the land for the Indigenous people, it only suggests that they have a right to use and occupy very small portions of it. Colonialism ensures that there is a definitive split between the European and Indigenous societies by defining the terms of land ownership according to a Eurocentric model. This model clearly favours the European position and ensures that a Eurocentric culture is the dominant culture while offering a stipend of land use to Indigenous people pursuant to the definition and terms of colonialism.

Eurocentric standpoint of colonialism

> *By promising the Indigenous people a minimum social safety net such as medicine, housing, food and a token recognition of culture, governments can now advance their colonial agenda of taking natural resources and opening the borders to non-Indigenous people.*

The 1763 Royal Proclamation set this standard when it specified that the Crown will be completely responsible for the Indigenous people by declaring them Loyal subjects entitled to protection by the Monarch. This set the stage for land and resource appropriation while promising that Indigenous people will never have to be responsible for their own future survival, but could have access to small bits of land to hunt and fish for traditional and personal purposes. The Crown and their European occupiers had the most to gain out of this deal and all they had to do in return was offer some minuscule promises that were nothing more than government welfare: government welfare designed to keep the Indigenous people dependant on government so that they can be controlled easier. Welfare is essentially nothing more than a perverse incentive that allows the recipients to remain under the control of government and prevents the recipients from advancing their traditional culture and or way of life. By promising the Indigenous people a minimum social safety net such as medicine, housing, food and a token

---

[6] https://quakerservice.ca/news/indigenous-land-rights-canada/
[7] https://www.thecanadianencyclopedia.ca/en/article/indigenous-territory

recognition of culture, governments can now advance their colonial agenda of taking natural resources and opening the borders and welcoming non-Indigenous people as citizens. All the government has to do is adhere to any treaties in order to meet the bare necessities promised to the Indigenous people. Treaties between European colonizers and Indigenous people have been numerous and have all been used to exchange a gratuity of land and a promise of provisions for the overall right of the Crown to control the land and resources as they see fit. While the colonial government takes the natural resources from underneath the Indigenous people, the government can meanwhile claim that they are the protectors of the Indigenous people because they provide them with compensation of welfare benefits disguised as *protection.* The European occupiers therefore had no problem whatsoever justifying their colonization of Indigenous lands and reaping the benefits of the natural resources it held. This falls completely inline with Noam Chomsky's view that colonialism is purely meant to benefit the financial interests of the foreign occupiers at the cost of the Indigenous people. But ironically enough, the European occupiers have claimed through the Royal Proclamation that they only acted in the best interest of the Indigenous people and that the protection of them was paramount. European centrism has dictated that white colonialism is the best thing for the Indigenous people simply because the European occupiers are the only ones who can properly develop and utilize the natural resources of the land. Because capitalistic trade and commerce was not part of the Indigenous culture, the European occupiers felt that this gave them the unequivocal right to solely take what resources they desired in the name of gaining profit. In order to do this they had to conquer land, and the more land they conquered, the greater access to natural resources they would have.

The European occupiers surmised that because the Indigenous people weren't using a specific area of land at that particular moment, it therefore gave them the right to capture it and develop it for their own benefit and this was clearly the case as far as the European common law system of land ownership was concerned. This school of colonial thought resulted in major social displacements for the Indigenous people; social displacements that rippled through generations and is still felt today in so many Indigenous communities. European occupiers took a passive aggressive approach to colonization by meting out parcels of land that the Indigenous people could call their own and use it for traditional purposes. In return the Indigenous people would essentially swear allegiance to the Crown who would then claim to be their protectors. Treaties were the promises that would begin a process of getting the Indigenous people dependent on the Crown for their very own survival. The Crown ensured that the immigration policies allowed many more Europeans to immigrate to the colonized lands and establish their affirmation as citizens in accordance to white colonial laws.

Indigenous lands and its resources

> *It might be considered ironic how advocating for the development of natural resources might be considered an inherent right, but if it's to be considered an inherent right then it should most definitely be the right of the Indigenous people to development them if they so desire.*

As mentioned by Noam Chomsky and his take on colonialism – where he suggests that reaping the resources of the land is a driving factor – today's Indigenous people have much more to say regarding the development of Canadian resources on or near their assigned reserve lands. This power has allowed many Indigenous people to oppose resource development citing concerns for the lands and the potential environmental implications of such developments. Stories where Indigenous groups oppose the development of oil, gas, mining or other natural resource development are prominent in the mainstream news, but this only tells one side of the narrative. The mainstream media always likes to suggest that there is a victim and villain when it comes to issues of natural resources and Indigenous people. This narrative could be due to the fact that the Canadian Indigenous people have suffered at the hands of past colonial policies that pillaged their resources, but now modern times have mandated that Indigenous people must have a stake in the development of resources that might negatively impact them. The negative effects of resource development make a great news story about victimization and how a socially disadvantage group is impacted by the corporate greed of non-Indigenous business people who are looking to plunder resources that aren't theirs in the first place. People seem to be drawn towards the fight of an underdog and that's why news stories that have a connotation suggesting an inequity of some sorts will grab the headlines. So when Indigenous people oppose the development of resources by a big corporation, it's easy to surmise that the said development would cause undue hardship toward the Indigenous people on top of the past harm they suffered due to colonialism. But what happens when Indigenous people actually support the development of natural resources and also has the business wherewithal to do so?

This is the case in northern Alberta where Indigenous people want to see the construction and use of an oil pipeline to allow oil to be transported out of the province and eventually to international markets. The Region One Aboriginal

Business Association is protesting the fact that they can only access the United States market for the sale of their oil and want to see the federal and provincial governments support a local pipeline. The ROABA have advocated that the oil and gas industry in Alberta has had a positive impact on Indigenous people and non-Indigenous alike. The ROABA believes that it's virtually an inherent right to develop the natural resources of the lands and vigorously oppose the federal government's Bill C-69 which would overhaul the way energy projects undergo approval.[8] It might be considered ironic how advocating for the development of natural resources could be considered an inherent right, but if it's to be considered an inherent right then it should most definitely be the right of the Indigenous people to develop them if they so desire. Unfortunately we can see an example of contemporary colonialism through the actions of the federal government by enacting Bill C-69 and inhibiting the natural resource development process thus demonstrating how the government dictates what it feels is best for the Indigenous people just as they historically have done for centuries.

Governments at all levels are infamous for dictating what is best for the Indigenous people and this has been reflected in the immigration policies that they've enacted. Immigration policies that resemble past colonialism – where the government used legislation to allow white settlers to benefit from Indigenous lands – is a prime example of the government arbitrarily deciding what is best for one group at the expense of another: in this case it's at the expense of the Indigenous people, their lands and their resources. The issue of contemporary immigration into Canada is something that will have an impact on all natural resources, especially petroleum products. It's obvious that in a cold climate like Canada there is a necessity for heat and the vast majority of that heat will come from oil and gas. The more people that come to Canada to settle, the more those settlers will need to keep their homes warm. On top of the heating issue is housing: the more people who come to Canada, the more of a need for natural resources such as timber to build houses and the land that goes with it. Despite how modern immigration programs increase the need for the use of more natural resources and how modern immigration is a mirror image of past colonialism in this respect, it's important to keep in mind how European colonialism centuries ago still has an impact on Indigenous people today.

The trauma of colonialism

> *The Indigenous people are then burdened with the social imbalances resulting from the inequities of a white settler society, meanwhile, the white settlers create a governmental bureaucracy to deal with it essentially acting as the hero and saviour.*

[8]https://www.cbc.ca/news/canada/edmonton/rally-lac-la-biche-1.5012585

Colonialism has been devastating on Canada's Indigenous people resulting in a high suicide rate[9], high drug abuse rate[10] and an over representation in the criminal justice system.[11] On top of this, Indigenous people are also more likely to be high school dropouts and more likely to be victims of crime.[12] The high school dropout rate for Indigenous people in Canada is over forty percent while the dropout rate for non-Indigenous people is around fifteen percent.[13] This disparity can be contributed to many factors that result from colonialism where the devastation is especially rampant among young Indigenous people who end up suffering social hardships. Drug abuse has been a major impediment for Indigenous people resulting in their over representation in the criminal justice system. Drug abuse and crime go hand-and-hand and are one of the main reasons why so many Indigenous people become involved with the criminal justice system. Drug related crimes often involve theft, robbery, distribution of narcotics and violence. Correctional institutions will then house a greater number of Indigenous people who often are repeat offenders as a result. There is a revolving door concept for Indigenous people relating to incarceration levels and their involvement in the criminal justice system as a whole whereas many Indigenous people have multiple experiences with the justice system from the time they're very young.[14] This negative involvement at younger ages usually starts when young Indigenous people are criminally victimized and then follows with drug abuse thus leading to criminal activity. Indigenous youth will disproportionately end up in young offenders facilities after negative experiences with the criminal justice system; and drug use is a major cause of this. The drug abuse often stems from the fact that Indigenous people are more likely to be victims of crime that see women and girls disproportionately affected by various forms of abuse often occurring at a young age. The decision to use and abuse drugs is thought to be a result of criminal victimization that can often be linked to colonialism.[15]

---

[9] https://www150.statcan.gc.ca/n1/pub/99-011-x/99-011-x2019001-eng.htm

[10] https://www.heretohelp.bc.ca/aboriginal-mental-health-statistical-reality

[11] https://www.justice.gc.ca/eng/rp-pr/jr/jf-pf/2017/jan02.html

[12] https://www.justice.gc.ca/eng/rp-pr/cj-jp/victim/rd3-rr3/p3.html

[13] http://newsactivist.com/en/articles/flacks-contemporary-issues-newsactivist-fall-2017/why-are-dropout-rates-higher-aboriginal

[14] http://www.csc-scc.gc.ca/research/r134-eng.shtml

[15] https://theindependent.ca/2015/10/08/the-colonial-roots-of-mental-health-and-addiction-among-indigenous-peoples-in-canada/

Physical, sexual and emotional abuse are something that many Indigenous women have endured at a young age and that's the reason why so many of them end up on the streets, homeless and drug addicted.[16] When Indigenous women end up living on the streets it's only a matter of time before they wind up becoming involved in the criminal justice system. Indigenous men are also over represented in the penal system, which sees up to a quarter of its population being Indigenous. Their involvement in the system often begins with simple police contact that arbitrarily targets Indigenous men for meagre reasons. These insufficient reasons can result in criminal charges ranging from public intoxication, possession of narcotics to a whole assortment of accusations. Once inside the penal system, Indigenous men face hardships that contribute to the further oppression and prevents them from being rehabilitated.[17] It's not only the penal system where Indigenous people are over represented, it's also the fact that they are also more likely to be victims of crimes.[18] Indigenous people face higher rates of suicide that is often double the national average in Canada. Many Aboriginal communities have been plagued by high suicide rates leading some to declare a state of emergency. Colonialism is often to blame and the evidence suggest that current governmental policies are a contributing factor. Indigenous reserves in Canada are often isolated from mainstream society and suffer the highest suicide rates. The hypothesis that colonialism created the Indigenous reserve system – so as to be on the fringes of society – is what drives the high suicide rate because Indigenous people are intentionally displaced from mainstream society.[19] Drug use, suicide, lack of schooling and negative involvement with the criminal justice system are issues that create a social trauma, and that trauma is attributed to colonialism.[20] Colonialism has created a trauma that has perpetuated the over representation of these issues, and these issues are an extreme burden on contemporary society. The social imbalance these issues create are a black eye on Canada's history and a clear indication that the white settler society is designed to advance only those who are beneficiaries to it. The Indigenous people are then burdened with the social imbalances resulting from the inequities of a white settler society, meanwhile, the white settlers create a governmental bureaucracy to deal with it essentially acting as the hero and saviour. This is where we begin to see the urgency of the white folks who proclaim to act as the social justice warriors for the Indigenous people who are suffering at the hands of the white European establishment to begin with.

---

[16] https://www.thestar.com/news/canada/2017/10/27/mmiw-inquiry-urged-to-speak-to-indigenous-women-in-prison.html

[17] https://theconversation.com/broken-system-why-is-a-quarter-of-canadas-prison-population-indigenous-91562

[18] https://www.justice.gc.ca/eng/rp-pr/jr/jf-pf/2017/jan02.html

[19] https://www.thecanadianencyclopedia.ca/en/article/suicide-among-indigenous-peoples-in-canada

[20] http://www.icad-cisd.com/pdf/Publications/Indigenous-Harm-Reduction-Policy-Brief.pdf

Besides the white folks who claim to advocate for the best interest of the Indigenous people, there are also those white folks who actually justify colonialism as something historically positive thus creating a dangerous situation either way.

Chapter 2:
Dangerous white men and their politics.

> The white man can now proudly pronounce that he has achieved control over his occupied lands and that everyone is content and benefiting from the newfound benevolence bestowed upon his racial and cultural subordinates.

The white man's politics is an interesting thing because it's the very politics that is used in contemporary society to offer protection for the Indigenous people, while at the same time, pronouncing Canada as a multicultural society that gains strength through diversity. The politics offered by the white man begins with taking the land and resources, building a modern infrastructure, providing tools of modernization to the Indigenous people and then segregating the Indigenous people to an assigned area away from the developed colonial establishment that consists of non-Indigenous people. Taking the land and the resources from the Indigenous people is self-explanatory but, providing modern tools such as hunting and cooking materials only serves to strip them of their traditional ways and forces them to become dependent on the colonial powers. The peculiarity behind the white man's politics is that the *system* will admit it was wrong and that it caused great harm and hardship to the Indigenous people while then initiating further political policies that will push Indigenous people even further into the trap of colonialism. It's as if the *system* is purposefully designed to ensure that it keeps repairing itself by a means of self-perpetual circular reasoning whereas it inflicts harm to a group of people but then makes an amends by inflicting a new harm. This new harm is disguised as something that will benefit the group who has been harmed. And yes it will sometimes come with a shallow apology or an indirect inference that there was minimal harm done to the group in the first place and that this will not happen again. In reality, this is only a means of gaining further control by assuring that the group of people harmed are then dependent on the political *system* that harmed them in the first place. The white man can now proudly pronounce that he has achieved control over his occupied lands and that everyone is content and benefiting from the newfound benevolence bestowed upon his racial and cultural subordinates. Benevolence such as roads, schools, transportation, healthcare and other ancillary social comforts that are privy to the white man's world in which wealth and success are the primary culmination of it all. Indigenous people have their little stipend of assigned lands, that they are segregated to, along with treaties and official recognition inside the supreme law of the land known as the Constitution, which offers a form of social equality that can only be justified as a success by someone who benefits from it: and this would be the white man of course. But how could and why would the white man benefit from making amends toward the Indigenous people? Those reasons are bountiful and mostly always political and are usually hijacked in a socially virtuous manner by those folks wishing to display a principled stance on social equity by viewing Canadian society through the lens of oppressor versus oppressed.

Dead white men

Contemporary Eurocentrism influences history by painting a picture of how the Indigenous people were conquered in North America and how the conquering was actually a benefit to them as opposed to something harmful. Scholars who rely on an interpretation of European based history will contend that the Indigenous people were treated respectfully and were allies of the Crown. This version of events can be disputed due to the Eurocentric bias that is aimed at justifying actions that resulted in the oppression of the Indigenous people. The *dead white men* (DWM) concept dictates that history was written from a racially white Eurocentric standpoint in order to create the persona that the European occupiers were necessary for the survival and livelihood of the Indigenous people. This tactic limits the guilt that should've resulted from colonialism and adds a *feel-good* element to the entire national history. An example of this tactic is how historians suggest that European technology was a great benefit to the Indigenous people because it allowed them the ability to gain a knowledge of European commerce thereby allowing them a better quality of life. Harold Innis wrote in his book, *The Fur Trade in Canada*, that the Indigenous people were middlemen in the fur trade between Europe and Canada and were locked into a network were they were primary collectors of a world economy. This was certainly possible due to European technology and logistics that allowed the Indigenous people to be an integral part of world trade. It also allows for a great deal of minimization for the suffering that the Indigenous people experienced due to colonialism and the loss of their land.

Another popular DWM concept often espoused by Eurocentric history is that the Indigenous people were allies of the Crown during the war of 1812 with The United States of America. It was believed by the Indigenous people at the time that Great Britain was the lesser of the two evils and that American colonization would do greater harm to the Indigenous way of life. This resulted in a convenient alliance between Great Britain, Métis and Many First Nations people in hopes of resisting American encroachment.[21] Unfortunately after the war, many Indigenous people lost what little self-reliance and self-determination they had left therefore demonstrating that history can often be selective when viewed from a European standpoint. The feel good stories of how the Indigenous people were an integral part of building the contemporary European based society is merely a sidestepping designed to distract away from the actual harm that colonialism did to the Indigenous people and their way of life. In all reality, today's Canadian society is one that is still very reminiscent of whiteness and Eurocentrism despite all the treaties, court ruling, apologies and promises made to the Indigenous people and this can be witnessed through the contemporary immigration policies.

Dead white men is a term that is ubiquitous among the critics of western societies where they surmise that the entire makeup of all western societies are inherently racist. The inherent racism stems from the sole fact that all founding principles, traditions and cultural practices are designed to benefit the white man. This includes the founding constitutions which are the backbone of modern individual freedoms and which have offered the most opportunities for all people to pursue their dreams. Indeed the constitutions of Canada and the United States were developed by white men and are written in such a way that they can be interpreted as being Eurocentric. Despite the accusation of Eurocentric influence within the Constitution, there has never been another country in the world that has offered so many people of many different races an enshrined guarantee of equality. Attacking Canadian society as being deficient when it comes to equality, because the constitution was developed by white men, is simply a method of fragmenting society into collective groups that are racialized and then victimized due to racism. This victimization is then said to be the result of the dead white men who intentionally designed a document that purposely oppressed non-whites by ensuring that the balance of governmental and social power stayed with the white European demographic. It's therefore easy to contend that the current constitutions are antiquated and should be considered obsolete and unenforceable, therefore giving credence to the social justice advocates who demand that contemporary society concede its alleged inherent racist intentions.

---

[21] https://www.thecanadianencyclopedia.ca/en/article/first-nations-in-the-war-of-1812

The idea that dead white men founded a nation that was specifically designed to oppress non-whites and specifically advance whites is a notion that stems from how the concept of western canon is a white-male based standard that all society must be measured by. Western canon is a collection of western literature that extends across a Eurocentric spectrum and holds philosophical concepts that appear to support a European standard of existence. Refuting this notion is a simple process that can be undertaken through applying critical theory by suggesting that western canon is rooted in whiteness and therefore inherently racist. The inherent racism can be simply concluded on the basis that it was white men who initially drafted the constitutional writing that became a benchmark for all civilized societies to adhere to. Critiquing everything from the standpoint of race is a very simplistic and an elementary way to convey a position that sounds noble and virtuous and is regularly done by intellectuals, scholars, students and politicians alike.

Essentially implying that classical literature works authored by dead white men were intentionally meant to oppress non-white people is an angle of philosophical attack that sets the stage for the deconstruction of the entire white settler society and institution. Laws, regulations, policies and the social structure of a white settler society can now be criticized and considered racist and in immediate need of an entire overhaul or revolution that would see racial equity implemented by removing any and all reminiscent of white Eurocentrism. This inevitably includes the founding constitutions that were drafted and implemented entirely by white men who died centuries ago and acknowledging that the importation of European immigrants caused grave harm to the Indigenous people. There's absolutely no doubt that the founding constitutions of the United States and Canada were drafted entirely by white men and no doubt that initial European immigration had adverse effects on the Indigenous people of North America. But simply critiquing the Constitution and suggesting that it is inherently racist is a flaccid abstraction. Just because the authors were white and the historical era was Eurocentric doesn't mean that changing it would somehow bring about amelioration. Suggestions for changes have only been lip service from social justice activists who ironically advocate open borders without giving consideration that any and all contemporary immigration into Canada and the United States is exactly the same as it was centuries ago: it's simply a tool used to colonize the lands with non-Indigenous people. Colonial immigration was used and justified as a means to build a nation and to provide a future for succeeding generations: and this is the mantra of contemporary immigration named multiculturalism where we are constantly reminded that this country was built by immigrants and that we must continue large scale immigration for ongoing success despite all the harm colonialism has caused the Indigenous people.

Despite how the interdisciplinary scholars, academics and students all refute colonialism and any positive influences it may have had on Indigenous people, many of these very same interdisciplinary scholars, academics and students praise multiculturalism as the be all and end all solution to an inherently racist colonial based society. These scholars, academics and students all proudly endorse multiculturalism as an equitable solution to the inherent problem of colonial racism while conveniently ignoring how the main component of multiculturalism is immigration. Immigration, no matter the historical era, has always been about the importation of non-Indigenous people into Indigenous lands for the sole purpose of using the lands for their own benefit. Changing the constitutions to reflect a more contemporary version of a multicultural/multi-ethnic society would still fail to ameliorate the many injustices that Indigenous people suffered at the hands of colonialism and its immigration policies. Furthermore, continuing the programs of immigration at a large scale would still solely amount to further colonization if colonization was interpreted as the occupation of Indigenous lands by non-Indigenous people. The term DWM is also applicable to how dangerous the white person can be and how past colonial policies can be reignited and totally justified under the semblance of racial equity and renamed to *multiculturalism.*

Dangerous white men and their benignity

> *"But the white liberals are foxes, who also show their teeth to the Negro but pretend that they are smiling. The white liberals are more dangerous than the conservatives; they lure the Negro, and as the Negro runs from the growling wolf, he flees into the open jaws of the "smiling" fox. One is the wolf, the other is a fox. No matter what, they'll both eat you."* (Malcom X)

Malcom X cleverly stated that white liberals are cunning and only wish to advance their own political agenda by appearing to be sympathetic to the cause of the racial minority. The term *liberal* is used by Malcom X to describe the Democrat Party of the United States, while at the same time making no qualms about how the *conservatives* (The Republican Party) are just as implicit, but also make no effort to hide their racism and bigotry under a cunning semblance of compassion. The take away from Malcolm X is that it's the white man who pretends to be compassionate about the plight of the racial minority – in which it willfully oppressed for its own benefit through colonialism – but who is actually very dangerous and the the least to be trusted. Malcom X highlights the fact that it's the white liberal who claims to be the one that can help solve the problems for the racial minorities, but in reality, the white person is actually the one who is part of the social mechanism that maintains the racial oppression that causes negative issues for non-whites.

What Malcom X essentially contends is that the white person who maintains a system of racial oppression – while claiming to offer assistance to those harmed by it – should be scoffed at for their ironic and obvious behaviour that clearly demonstrates covert racism. The white liberal can therefore certainly be an elusive creature to gauge, when you consider their strong outward appearance of compassion and their strong outward belief of social inclusiveness, social justice and social equity. Indeed the white liberal is perhaps the strongest proponent of Indigenous rights in Canada and the most vocal when it comes to suggesting that this land belongs to the Indigenous people; only proving in the end to be paradoxical in their own righteousness. Taking the position of Malcom X and how he believes that the white liberal is cunning in their noble political posture, it's clear that a paradox has occurred when contemplating how the white liberal advocates open borders through multiculturalism, while at the same time, claiming to be a champion for Indigenous people, their rights, their lands and their resources.

Malcom X famously said that white liberals profess to be a friend of black people while eloquently comparing white liberals to foxes who cunningly pretend to be friends with lambs then end up with lamp chops on their plates. Malcom X went on to say that foxes, unlike wolves, pretend to be friends but want the same end result as wolves. Foxes therefore are more dangerous due to their cunning nature just like white liberals who represent the interest of the white political elites by pretending to be compassionate about racial equality.[22] Professor and writer Robin DiAangelo has written extensively about whiteness and racial inequality and suggests that whiteness is a major influence on contemporary North American society. This major influence of whiteness is highlighted by the fact that DiAangelo believes that all white people have an inherent set of privileges that entitle them to unearned and automatic social benefits. These social benefits allow whites to enjoy a greater lifestyle in which society recognizes, respects and upholds whiteness through white

---

[22] https://youtu.be/ZjS0ZVa8oyl

principles. This is where, how and why the element of whiteness is disguised through cunningness and is used to explain how colonialism is covertly being maintained in modern society through the use of social virtue. Social virtue dressed as a white person who asserts that Canada is a nation built by immigrants and that immigration is necessary in order to sustain Canada's identity and global image. *Dangerous white men* are instrumental in establishing a collective concept that encourages further colonialism by cleverly disguising their platform to appear to be based on social justice and social equity. The *DWMs* of the world are infamous for sitting around the campfire and singing kumbaya and believing that their social righteousness will save them from the sins of their whiteness. The *DWM* is a funny and contradictory creature whereas they are quick to espouse how the whites invaded and stole Indigenous lands and resources, while at the same time, encouraging open borders and mass immigration through the guise of multiculturalism.

Chapter 3:
Multiculturalism equals immigration but can multiculturalism be colonialism?

> *The paradoxical nature of multiculturalism is that it can't exist without immigration, just the same as European colonialism can't exist without immigration.*

This Land is Your Land is the original multicultural song that rocked the free world decades ago and highlighted the meaning of social cohesion and international love from the perspective of the social justice warrior. The song clearly implies that the world shouldn't have any borders and that all people are citizens of the world and all people should live in harmony. There's nothing wrong with this idea whatsoever as it essentially implies world peace. The issue is that the song also implies that there won't be any world peace unless international borders are extinguished and unless everyone embraces their fellow citizen as an equal person regardless of race, religion, creed and any other distinguishing individual factors. In other words; white settler societies should halt their racist ways and acknowledge that remorse can be expressed through racial equity and this equity can only be achieved via open borders: an open border where all people are equal citizens of a free society that is socially cohesive and where all people can freely remain attached to their cultural and religious identity. By encouraging people to remain attached to their cultural and religious identity – while expressing that the land is as much theirs as yours – equality will undoubtedly be achieved and humans will live in harmony. Well despite the feel-good tone of this idea, one has to ask the Indigenous people if they feel good about the colonialism they endured when colonial policies opened up the borders to the white settlers and suggested that everyone simply live in harmony. I somehow highly doubt that your everyday Indigenous person will concur that they feel real good in a sing-song kind of way about open borders, global citizenry and the notion that peace will be achieved through such feel-good concepts.

This is a prime example of how the white liberal can be cunning and paradoxical in their perspective on social equality and the political means to attain it, and it's exemplified when they espouse their support for multiculturalism. The paradoxical nature of multiculturalism is that it can't exist without immigration, just the same as European colonialism couldn't exist without immigration. Simply put: a key component of colonialism is immigration because it's immigration that sets the stage for the seizure of lands and resources from the Indigenous people in order to satisfy the material needs of the settlers. Multiculturalism exclusively involves immigration in order to establish its social dominance in contemporary society thereby making it a pronounced version of contemporary colonialism. Just like the original European colonialism that initiated the theft of land and resources from the Indigenous people, multiculturalism ensures that the continuation of such theft continues in modern times in order to meet the material needs of contemporary settlers. Needs such as housing and the property it requires and the natural resources to meet the energy consumption are just a small part of the necessities of an increasing contemporary population. This modern appropriation of land and resources – disguised as diversity through strength and called multiculturalism – is completely endorsed by all levels of governments and is based on an open border concept that allows virtually anyone to establish their claim to a Canadian citizenship in the same way as past colonial immigration policies encouraged mass immigration and a claim to Canadian land and resources. Multiculturalism is therefore a multi-faceted concept that includes all methods of obtaining citizenship and is celebrated as a crowning achievement for governments and dangerous white people who profess time and time again that Canada is a country of immigrants that was built by immigration and that immigration must be ever continuous. Contemporary immigration advocates constantly declare that ongoing immigration is necessary in order for Canada to sustain itself and that Canada is a wide open country with lots of space. The lots of space issue is something that demonstrates just how cunning social justice advocates can be when they justify their desire for immigration based off the premise that there's plenty of land space in Canada to potentially house new immigrants. This is something that will be discussed later in the book.

Features of a white settler society and its relation to post-colonial immigration

Some key features of a white settler society are: settler colonizers come to stay on their newly gotten lands; second, settler colonization is a structure and not an event because settlers intend on eliminating the Indigenous population; third, settler colonization has a goal of ending colonial differences and establishing a supreme and unchallenged settler-state.[23] Examining this premise it is clearly safe to conclude that indeed the white European settlers occupied Indigenous lands for the purpose of forming a white European society that was specifically designed to place the Indigenous people to assigned corners of the social and political structure and ensure that they remain there via white structured laws and the enforcement of such laws. Applying this premise to multiculturalism, and other forms of post-colonial immigration, it's safe to suggest that multiculturalism, the foremost common method of post-colonial immigration, fits the criteria of all three mentioned features.

Firstly: Immigrants who come to Canada under the terms of multiculturalism come to stay and permanently settle as citizens in a post-colonial society that embraces diversity as its strength and as a prominent component of its national identity and contemporary culture. Even refugees who claim to be fleeing imminent persecution are granted full citizenship or permanent residency (that soon leads to full citizenship) upon arrival on Canadian soil or even when granted Canadian citizenship at refugee camps abroad. Despite the United Nations definition of a refugee being someone who needs temporary safety in the first safe country they find, Canada will actually dole out citizenship notwithstanding the fact that many refugees never return to their original country when it becomes safe to do so. Refugees are encouraged by the government to make Canada their permanent home and settle into the post-colonial contemporary society as an indefinite social characteristic. Indeed multiculturalism and other forms of post-colonial immigration have created and shaped Canadian society to be one that consists of a new version of non-Indigenous settlers just the same as the white Europeans were centuries ago.

---

[23] https://globalsocialtheory.org/concepts/settler-colonialism/

Secondly: Multiculturalism creates a social structure where cultural and racial diversity is paramount in defining what Canada's identity is and results in massive amounts of immigration that increases the need for more land, natural resources and government recognition of the diversity it subsequently produces. Although this aspect doesn't directly eliminate the Indigenous population, it certainly assists in pushing the Indigenous people into a social category that only defines them as being part of an overall ethnic and cultural minority group. They are basically the same as their multicultural counterparts when viewed from the standpoint of how Canada is defined as a contemporary nation. Indigenous people are essentially eliminated from the historical significance they contributed to the country, they are eliminated from their attachment to the land and natural resources and they are eliminated from the mainstream society that must continue to encroach further and further outward to accommodate the increasing numbers of contemporary settlers entering the country.

Thirdly: Multiculturalism becomes the defining factor that is the foundational aspect of the country's identity and it requires a large degree of government enforcement. Implementing multiculturalism is also an excellent means for government to bypass the established colonial structure and erase its racist white based composition that was used to oppress the Indigenous people since its inception. Bypassing the old colonial structure with multiculturalism can create the illusion that past injustices against Indigenous people are now forgiven and forgotten because the new post-colonial immigration – disguised as multiculturalism – is one that consists of no *whiteness* being enforced on society and that the old enforcement of *whiteness* is now replaced with racial and cultural diversity. This means that the reminiscences of colonialism is presumed to be entirely erased and replaced with a system of complete racial equity; when in reality, it's just another government program initiated by a system that was founded on a colonial structure built by white people. Post-colonial immigration is still the immigration of non-Indigenous people that will require the use of the land, the resources and the services of the government; just the same as white colonialism did centuries ago.

Perpetual whiteness

Whiteness is synonymous with colonialism in terms of how colonialism, as an ideology, suggests that society must represent itself as being white and all aspects of society must reflect this accordingly. Whiteness is said to be engrained into a system designed to ensure that all whites receive an inherent set of privileges that help ensure a hierarchy where non-whites are systemically oppressed.[24] It can be argued that colonialism ensures that this system of whiteness will continue throughout successive governments and generations thus preserving its identity, existence and power. Simply put: whiteness is the very structure that results from a society colonized by white people and it is what has created the imbalance of societal power; hence the reason why contemporary Canadian society, and other colonial white settler societies, are rife with racism and racial inequity – according to social justice advocates who champion open borders. This concept can however be considered a subjective one, but when someone questions the accusations of social imbalances due to whiteness, they too are categorized as being part of the problem and not part of the solution. The entire concept of whiteness can be used to explain almost every problem in contemporary Canadian society relating to how racial inequities are omnipresent and creating insurmountable barriers for non-whites. In a nutshell, whiteness essentially dictates that Canadian society was founded on principles that were cleverly drafted in order to elevate whites into a permanent position of power and privilege, while at the same time, guaranteeing that non-whites were at the bottom of this power structure. The simple remedy to this – so in theory – is the complete dismantling of society from the top-down and then a complete rebuilding from the bottom-up to ensure an equal power distribution. The concept of multiculturalism is one potential possibility that can restructure a white settler society thus making it less like an occupied colonial establishment. Until this happens however, whiteness can be considered *perpetual* regardless of what measures are taken to address any social inequities that may relate to a racial imbalance.

Non white whiteness

It's evidently clear that whiteness is synonymous with colonialism, but is it possible for whiteness to be a stand alone ideology existing without the presence of white people? According to the definition of whiteness described above, it takes the actions of white people in order to initiate the concept of whiteness whereas the results will be the systemic and institutional oppression of non-whites. I would however suggest – rather boldly at this point do to a lack of academic research to support it – that the ideology of whiteness could also be perpetrated by non-whites, when the oppression relates to contemporary colonialism in the form of new

---

[24] http://www.aclrc.com/whiteness

settlers arriving in Canada further inhabiting already occupied lands and resources that once belonged to the Indigenous people. This contemporary colonialism happens through the settlement of new immigrants who take advantage of generous immigration and social programs that are all encouraged by the established white governments who proclaim that the country's national identity is one of multiculturalism. Essentially, new immigrants flock to Canada due to governmental encouragement that Canada is a nation that was built on immigration and this is the nation where a new immigrant can have an excellent quality of life and achieve virtually anything. This governmental encouragement comes from the notion that Canada is a multicultural nation that must adhere to diversity because this diversity makes the country strong. Tracing this notion of diversity as strength through multiculturalism can be credited to former Prime Minister Pierre Elliot Trudeau who coined the ideology that open borders demonstrate tolerance and inclusiveness.[25]

In order to justify an open border concept, government officials had to be unique in their sales pitch to white Canadians in such a way that it wouldn't threaten their whiteness that European colonialism had established and maintained for them. This was done through the simple hypothesis of multiculturalism. Multiculturalism was then conceived, implemented and maintained by a government that was virtually all white and it was successfully sold to Canadians as a program that would ensure Canada would be the the pride and joy of the free world by demonstrating diversity and inclusiveness. These white politicians developed this sales pitch through the theory that Canada would be a world leader in social equity and that Canada would then be the envy of the free world because it set a new standard for racial equality. This new deal was secured through the many unstinting immigration programs that have been the results of policies that have made immigration to Canada as easy as having the borders pretty much open. Policies that allow for the immediate acceptance of government sponsored refugees, Provincial Nominee Programs, the acceptance of asylum seekers who walk across the international border and government mandated employment programs that allow corporations instant access to foreign workers. There are also a whole host of other immigration policies and programs that allow for the private sponsorship of new immigrants to easily settle in Canada and gain citizenship. One of these most popular programs of private sponsorship of immigrants is the family reunification program.

---

[25]https://www.theglobeandmail.com/opinion/canadians-must-never-take-multiculturalism-for-granted/article30773630/

Family reunification allows Canadian citizens to sponser their relatives for settlement resulting in chain immigration where each new settler can then sponsor other family members and so-on. This program generates a substantial increase in contemporary settlers to Canada and is what politicians use as a base for promoting their ideology of multiculturalism and diversity as strength. This form of modern settlement is certainly a far cry from the old white European colonial programs of immigration, but it still amounts to a contemporary form of non-Indigenous settlement that was perpetrated by past governments, who were white, and who pronounced that they knew what would be best for Canada. Multiculturalism has all but replaced colonial immigration methods with the only difference being that the new settlers are non-white but still non-Indigenous nonetheless. The white governments/politicians who launched the concept of multiculturalism were successful in maintaining the white European goal of conquering, occupying and settling Indigenous lands with non-Indigenous people. The white governments/politicians successfully used non-white people as pawns in their game of contemporary colonialism to push Indigenous people even further away from mainstream society and away from their lands and resources thus making them nothing more than an oppressed racial minority that only the government can help. Even though the contemporary settlers are non-white, the Indigenous lands and resources are still being occupied in a white European colonial manner due to the fact that it is still being perpetrated by a government that was established through whiteness in the first place. Successive governments have ensured that white European colonial powers and ideology still rule supreme and that colonialism will continue so long as the land is occupied, controlled and maintained by non-Indigenous people therefore fortifying systemic and institutional whiteness within Canadian society.

Chapter 4: The Many Faces of Multiculturalism.

Multiculturalism, immigration, open borders and how it relates to contemporary colonialism

> *This concept would allow for the theoretical transformation of Canada from a white settler country into an egalitarian nation where all persons would have an equal shot at social equity.*

Multiculturalism entails the influx of non-European based cultures into Canada and it does so under government mandate. Since 1971, Canada has been an official importer of non-European cultures into the country in an effort to remake society into something that no longer resembles white European colonialism. In 1988, the Multiculturalism Act came into force with an aim to transform the cultural landscape into one that promotes a diverse kind of Canadian citizenship that entitles the holder to be an all inclusive Canadian while still holding onto their own cultural identity and even the citizenship to their native country. This fundamentally means that a citizen is no longer identified by the terms of Eurocentric white standards to be considered Canadian, they can be a person of colour who doesn't speak English or French and the government now has a duty to reasonably accommodate them accordingly. If a person's culture or religion requires them to adhere to non-European social standards or customs, the government then has a duty to ensure that those non-European social standards and customs are adhered to. This is where Canada's European whiteness, that is the cultural norm according to colonialism, would be transformed into a checkerboard of cultures and races living side-by-side with their white European counterparts. This concept would allow for the theoretical transformation of Canada from a white settler country into an egalitarian nation where all persons would have an equal shot at racial equity. Regardless of whether or not the non-European Canadian desires to be integrated into a white based society and speak one of the official languages, the non-white Canadian is just as Canadian as the white Canadian and this is what politicians consider to be a social success. Irene Bloemraad of the University of California at Berkeley believes that the Canadian multicultural experiment is a success after polls indicate that Canadians are proud of it and believe that it defines Canada's identity.[26]

This suggests that the vast majority of Canadians do believe that multiculturalism should be celebrated and that it's certainly something to be proud of in terms of a national identity. If indeed Bloemraad is correct in her suggestion that the more ethnically diverse Canada becomes the more happy Canadians should be, then the solution to all racial inequities should be *multiculturalism* therefore making Canada a true oasis of racial equality. The general consensus of intellectuals and academics in Canada is that multiculturalism is a positive social instrument and a net benefit for Canada as it defines Canada as an open and tolerant nation where many different cultures can live in harmony. Theoretically, this should dictate that racial and cultural differences shouldn't matter and that coexistence is the ultimate result of a multicultural society that was initially colonized by whites. This however is not completely accurate. While intellectuals and academia praise multiculturalism, they are also quick to point out that racism is a major issue in

---

[26] https://www.theglobeandmail.com/opinion/multiculturalism-has-been-canadas-solution-not-its-problem/article4330460/

Canada despite espousing the social tolerance that multiculturalism is said to provide.

As a white settler society, Canada has long standing traditions and customs that reflect whiteness, which is engrained into the very social fabric, so how could these engrained customs not conflict with cultural or ethnic practices that are not conducive with whiteness? Kogila Moodley describes Canadian multiculturalism as an ideology that neutralizes Indigenous people's land claims and forgotten treaties and only equalizes First Nations people among the *others* who fall under the multicultural spectrum.[27] The *others* can be defined as the racial others who are part of the Canadian multicultural setting and who are the benefactors of Canadian citizenship while they maintain their distinctive non-white identity. The mere fact that the *other* is granted the privilege to exist as racially distinct within a white settler society, and not required to assimilate, essentially means that they have special status bestowed upon them. Their special status that they hold is a default setting that automatically accompanies the theoretical concept of multiculturalism. The *other* is now defined as an integral part of the Canadian identity and has no obligation to be loyal to a Canada that resembles whiteness. Whiteness is of course the concept that is deemed to be bad due to the historical nature that represents the white settler society that makes up Canada's colonial identity. The end result to Moodley's standpoint is that Indigenous people receive no benefit from multiculturalism just as they received no benefit from colonialism because they are simply just another racialized non-white group used as tokens of diversity by governmental powers. If indeed Canada was true to this concept of coexistence between many different cultures as multiculturalism suggests – where they weren't required to conform to a white society – then each distinct group should be an independent part of society while still being an integral part of the entire sum. This however is not exactly true.

When a distinct culture within a white settler society wishes to integrate into one or more aspects of it while maintaining their own distinctness, an immediate conflict occurs. Take the example of orthodox Sikhs who assert that they have a right to maintain the cultural aspects of their dress for religious reason: requiring them to alter their dress to fit the traditions of a white settler society can be deemed as racist according to multiculturalism. This has already been witnessed a number of times in recent decades with orthodox Sikhs who wish to assert their religious right to wear their traditional attire. The same could be described with Islam and the requirement to pray five times a day and the requirement to adhere to many other

---

[27] Ethnic and Racial Studies Volume 6 Number 3 July 1983 R.K.P 1983 0141-9870/83/0603-0320 81.50.1

aspects of sharia law that are not conducive with a white settler society. The reason why these two examples show how the *other* can dominate the cultural identity of Canada is exemplified through the act of reasonable accommodation. If there is a need to accommodate a cultural group that is not required to assimilate then the accommodation itself is rather moot. The reason that most cultural groups are attracted to a multicultural society is that they aren't required to assimilate and that their acceptance as the *other* will be positive as opposed to negative. But when the *other* requires accommodation to be part of the society then it proves that the society itself has failed the *other*. This essentially means that multiculturalism is an ideology that has failed to provide a society where cultures live as a checkerboard with each culture occupying their own square in the board while still being part of the larger board itself; hence part of the larger sum. Instead, other squares representing different cultures are being required to accommodate the special needs of other cultures occupying neighbouring squares all in the name of achieving racial equality. So the concept of different cultures all living together harmoniously in a country where all cultures are considered equal is a myth. But multiculturalism is however an attractive tool for politicians, academics and intellectuals who all believe that there are no true limits to reasonable accommodation and this sets the stage for unlimited possibilities.

Professor Evelyn Kallen of York University once proposed that Canada actually become a multilingual country suggesting that all students be taught in their individual ancestral language.[28] This is a prime example of the checkerboard aspect of multiculturalism which essentially requires that no immigrant shall assimilate into a white settler society if they don't wish to do so. It's also an extreme example of multiculturalism that is highly unlikely to happen, but it does demonstrate the unchecked logic of academic intellectuals who are basically out of touch with mainstream scholastic thought. The mainstream scholastic thought within academia certainly advocates multiculturalism, open borders, mass immigration and the required accommodation that must accompany it, but there is still a general consensus that multiculturalism is intended to create some form of national harmony. If the extreme measures suggested by professor Kallen were actually considered, isolation amongst ethnic groups would certainly occur where communities would be virtually segregated with absolutely no hope of assimilation whatsoever. The requirement to undergo assimilation is a choice that immigrants should have under a moderate multicultural program, which is usually the option that most people would rather see.

---

[28] Stoffman, Daniel. (2002). *Who Gets In. What's wrong with Canada's immigration program-and how to fix it.* Macfarlane Water & Ross. Toronto p. 131

If extreme measures were taken to prevent the option of assimilation into a white settler society and the inevitable isolation did occur, then there would be no reason why the isolated communities shouldn't be able to practice whatever cultural traditions they so desired and be exempt from white colonial laws. Examples would be a Somalian community using the herb khat, which is an illegal substance in Canada because it contains LSD type ingredients; South Asians eating dog meat; African Muslims circumcising girls; Muslims implementing Sharia law that violate many equality aspects of the Canadian constitution relating to women's rights and allowing plural marriages within certain religions or cultures. The academics and intellectuals who espouse extreme multicultural measures, in the name of building a utopian society where all cultures are equal regardless of exotic cultural norms, often overlook the eminent reality of non-assimilation. Academics and intellectuals are content with extreme multicultural measures so long as the cultures aren't required to submit to the laws, customs or rules of a white settler society because the white settler society is essentially racist by default. How can academics and intellectuals embrace such extreme measures and justify creating a fragmented nation that is defined by collective groups who are then defined by culture? It's because the concept of multiculturalism is anti-colonial and anti-white settler society thereby making it an option to European colonialism.

The invention of multiculturalism

Multiculturalism is an invention that derives from the political philosophy that a white settler country will adopt a program that ignites racial equality through changing the spectrum of race. Multiculturalism is essentially the tool used by white people to deny racism and to allow them to display acts of social valour by pronouncing that they are not racist and that they can coexist with a variety of ethnicities. Multiculturalism is also an excellent tool for white folks to acknowledge that they are settlers on stolen land while allowing them to proclaim their reconciliation with the Indigenous people. As incongruous as this seems, it's the exact reason why you'll hear many white people endorse mass immigration while they acknowledge that the Indigenous people are the first to inhabit the lands and must therefore be respected as such and never forgotten as such. The reason why this incongruity arises is because colonialism has created a situation where lands have been stolen, occupied and developed solely to benefit the colonizers. At the same time, the colonizers constantly remind everyone that the land is stolen and that the Indigenous people have suffered greatly because of it, but that somehow being multicultural in their beliefs is a form of self-forgiveness. The connection between colonialism and multiculturalism is evident due to the fact that it's only countries colonized by white people that are so insistent on being multicultural. Implementing multiculturalism can only be done through programs of immigration that allow large numbers of newcomers to come to the already colonized lands. Mono-ethnic countries such as Japan, Saudi Arabia, Iran, North and South Korea and China don't practice multiculturalism as a form of social or racial equality, in fact mono-ethnic countries are usually very adherent to a national identity that is based off of their culture, religion and language. The entire concept of multiculturalism stems from countries like Canada, the United States, Australia and New Zealand who were all colonized by white people. The white people in these cases hailed from Europe, mainly Great Britain. Today we see that Great Britain and many other European countries are also adopting multiculturalism as an aspect of their national identity.

Great Britain was the primary white nation that historically made a valiant effort to have a presence in as many foreign countries as feasibly possible creating the expression, "the empire on which the sun never sets". Other white European countries such as Germany, the Netherlands, France and Scandinavian countries have also embraced multiculturalism as a means of creating racial diversity. The empire of Great Britain certainly occupied many lands around the world, but to their credit, they did implement some actions of decolonization in Africa and Asian which saw some lands and resources given back to its Indigenous people. The actions of decolonization from Great Britain was greeted with further programs of immigration to their own country and political encouragement of racial diversity as a token of tolerance and social inclusiveness. The same could be said for Germany who is best known for its horrible history of the Second World War and the Holocaust. It goes without saying that Germany once boasted itself as the nation of pure whiteness while intending to enforce this whiteness on the world as a political ideology. Fortunately this political ideology of whiteness was defeated and the concept of pure whiteness was defeated with it. Since then, Germany has been a world leader in implementing diversity and inclusiveness and has opened its doors to hundreds of thousands, if not millions, of people seeking a new way of life. To be German now means to be inclusive, open and tolerant while embracing other cultures as part of the national identity: much the same as Canada where immigration is touted as a key component of the national identity and history.

Necessary immigration: does it benefit the economy?

There is an argument that immigration is a net benefit to the economy and is absolutely necessary in order to create and sustain a way of life that promotes individual prosperity. All to often we hear immigration advocates claim that we need immigrants because they are the core factor in creating employment and contributing to the tax base. Immigration advocates constantly cite that immigrants are an essential component of diversity which somehow benefits the economy by allowing businesses to be more globally competitive. Yes there is some basis to this argument if consideration is given to the fact that immigrants can access their native country for the purpose of doing business with Canada. Immigrants who have access to business connections in their native country can often utilize those connections in order to conduct business successfully in Canada. Take the example of an immigrant who develops a service, such as a computer software program, and then promotes that service in their native country where they may already have existing market connections and have extensive knowledge of the culture and language. This would certainly ensure that a successful business could be launched from Canada, which would in return create the ability to generate corporate and personal tax income while potentially creating local employment. This idea however is not just a *what if*, it's actually a reality for many immigrants who choose Canada specifically for the purpose of international business. Immigrants who can contribute to the economy are definitely a net benefit and could fall under the category of *necessary* due simply to the fact that they are net givers and not net takers. The impression that is given by immigration advocates is that the only way for Canada's economy to thrive and survive is through immigration and therefore we must open the borders to ensure economic success regardless of who the immigrants are. Unfortunately this only tells one side of the *necessary* immigration story and doesn't take into consideration how every immigrant can't be a net contributor to the economy. If immigration was as simple as merely letting in people, and then miraculously the economy boomed into a flourishing fountain of wealth, why not inject as many immigrants as possible in the shortest period of time possible and then there'll be immediate success? This is the question that can't be answered by immigration advocates because the reality is that unrelenting immigration without consideration to specific economic needs will result in net takers and not net givers.[29] Again, immigration advocates always insist that immigration is completely necessary but they can't give a specific number to how many it would take in order to ensure that every Canadian would prosper. What you'll get instead from immigration advocates is the old adage that Canada has lots

---

[29] https://www.rcinet.ca/immigration-en/2017/03/08/immigration-a-30b-fiscal-burden-on-canadian-economy/

of space and room and that we should be welcoming as many immigrants as possible because it's a country that was built by immigration. The issue of exactly how many immigrants should be taken in, or how many are needed to increase the economy, is a point that immigration advocates can't answer because it shatters their utopian concept of economics. The only answer that can be given by advocates is that it's just necessary and that Canada is a country of immigrants after all.

But there's plenty of space for lots of people in Canada: right?

The issue of *space* when referring to immigrants is often anecdotally cited by immigration advocates as a reason for taking in large numbers of immigrants because Canada is a massive country with lots of empty land to house people. The logic behind this notion is rather flaccid simply because it implies that wherever there's empty space, such as an open field, wooded forest or any undeveloped piece of land, we should immediately fill it up with immigrants. How many times have you heard that argument? Well I've heard it a number if times and I've always thought that it doesn't hold water. There's no rhyme or reason why an open/empty field should be converted into a residence for immigrants solely because that open/empty field is sitting there empty. Mass immigration in the last two decades has created a major housing crisis resulting in overcrowded homeless shelters and a low vacancy rate for potential renters. The price of housing has also skyrocketed in major cities where wealthy immigrants have literally bought up properties well above the valued price.[30] This is possible when there is a housing crisis due to the fact that there are more people than places to live. Simply put: it's the laws of supply and demand. The winners in a supply and demand crisis are the ones with the money. The ones with the money can obviously outbid those with less monetary clout thus resulting in overpaying what a house is actually worth. This serves as an injustice for people who require affordable housing as it puts more strain on the rental market by depleting the availability of reasonably priced accommodations.[31]

Former Canadian Minister of Foreign Affairs and current chair of the World Refugee Council Lloyd Axworthy has strongly suggested that Canada should accept Central American migrants that are held up at the U.S. border. Axworthy believes that the province of Manitoba should set an example to the world by taking in as many refugees as possible. He contends that the province of Manitoba,

---

[30] https://www.sauder.ubc.ca/sites/default/files/2019-06/Immigration%20and%20Real%20Estate%20Returns.pdf
[31] https://nationalpost.com/news/canada/charlottetowns-housing-crisis

and Canada in general, is a big country with lots of space and that immigration has had a tremendous benefit for the economy. Axworthy speaks personally as a person from Winnipeg who has witnessed how diversity has been a positive social attribute that demonstrates how compassionate Manitobans are.[32] Whether Axworthy is speaking personally from the heart or whether he is speaking as chair of the World Refugee Council, it's a claim that many politicians make by citing the *space* issue which specifies that if there is *space* for immigrants then they should occupy it. This is clearly the same contention that European colonizers had when they felt it was prudent to occupy the Indigenous people's lands simply because they were empty at the time. Empty, unused or barren land was a major justification that European colonizers needed in order to stake their claim and establish a white settler society: the same white settler society we have today where politicians continue to stake claim to empty land and lots of *space*. Lloyd Axworthy's idea of empty *space* being the justification for accepting immigrants is completely inline with what the European colonizers had when they became the occupiers of Indigenous lands. The main difference today is that the Axworthys of the political arena use the concept of diversity as grounds to establish their agenda of contemporary colonialism. Diversity is the tool that is used to inflict accusations of racism: opposing diversity is deemed as an act of racism and being unpatriotic as it defies the political notion that diversity is strength. Politicians and immigration advocates such as Axworthy are eager to exploit the idea that contemporary immigration is a net benefit to Canadians and that diversity is completely inline with what Indigenous people desire. It's somehow supposed to be conceivable that Canada's cultural diversity creates a social mosaic that actually benefits Indigenous people and somehow erases the damage done by colonialism.

• • • • • • • • • • • • •

The Canadian Race Relations Foundation found that new immigrants to Canada quickly picked up on negative stereotypes about Indigenous people, but after exposure to Canadian society those stereotypes diminished rapidly. The quick diminishing of these stereotypes is said to come after new immigrants realize that they face the same employment issues as Indigenous people. The Kamloops Immigrant Services believe that once Indigenous communities realize that immigrants aren't taking work away from them and that immigrants struggle just as much as Indigenous people do finding work, a common social bond will somehow form between them making the contemporary settlers welcome as

---

[32] https://globalnews.ca/news/4764058/manitoba-should-welcome-migrants-stuck-at-us-mexico-border-says-axworthy/

Canadians. Both the Canadian Race Foundation and the Kamloops Immigrant Services suggest that Indigenous people and immigrants go hand and hand in establishing a cultural mosaic and that the two groups can learn to understand each other and how their individual struggles have many commonalities in a white settler society.[33]

Establishing commonalities between racial minorities in a white settler society is an easy way for politicians and advocates of multiculturalism to institute a political base that will enforce an agenda of *diversity as strength*. This agenda will easily allow for the continuation of mass immigration into what is perceived as empty or barren lands despite the fact that the lands have already been colonized by immigrants of the past and is still being colonized further with current immigrants. Multiculturalism can certainly allow for an obvious connection between Indigenous people and racial minorities as some immigrants may feel an overwhelming amount of whiteness due to European colonialism and how it's reflected in society. Critical race theory holds that the white structures within a European colonized society creates systemic and institutional barriers for non-whites, which could essentially pave the way for the alignment or social bond between all non-white people.[34] So the fact that the Indigenous lands were previously colonized by white Europeans is the only ammunition that multiculturalists and advocates of mass immigration need in order to sell contemporary colonialism through the open border concept. Multiculturalism is not the immigration of white European people, as it was in the past due to colonialism, so it can't necessarily be considered a bad form of immigration as far as the open border advocates are concerned. The connection between Indigenous people and new immigrants is then established and multiculturalism is fully justified and not an act of land theft or cultural destruction. The wide open land spaces can now be acquired and settled by new immigrants – who are racial minorities – in a show of solidarity against past colonial whiteness by celebrating diversity as strength.

Do non-Indigenous people have an inherent claim to settle on contemporary land?

The argument that vacant land, that is of no apparent use, is an object that can be used for the benefit of the person who discovers it is often cited as an explanation

---

[33] https://canadianimmigrant.ca/living/community/the-connection-between-immigrants-and-aboriginal-people-in-canadas-mosaic

[34] https://owl.purdue.edu/owl/subject_specific_writing/writing_in_literature/literary_theory_and_schools_of_criticism/critical_race_theory.html

for occupying such lands. Using this premise to infer that there is an inherent right for white European settlers to occupy and use vacant lands for their own benefit is precisely what colonizers did centuries ago. Believing that unused lands are something for the taking, just because they are not occupied, is the guiding force for all colonial activity. Colonizers have operated under this modus operandi since their first contact with Indigenous people and the first seizure of Indigenous lands occurred. Suggesting that someone could justify the seizure of lands because they are vacant is blatantly arrogant in today's society and would surely result in instant litigation that would favour the true land owner. Colonizers however found justification in their motives by contending that Indigenous people would often expropriate the lands of other tribes who were weaker or perceived inferior to them. Colonizers also justified their actions by citing that the Indigenous people also believed that vacant/unused lands were for the taking so long as they were uninhabited and so long as the land could be put to use in some way.[35] There are however those who feel that non-Indigenous people do have a claim to North American land due to a distant blood relationship to it.

American politician Alexandria Ocasio-Cortez suggested that the United States owes it to the Central American caravan of migrants who were seeking settlement in the United States because they are actually Native to America. Ocasio-Cortez stated that she would defund Immigration and Customs Enforcement (ICE) and ensure that all Latino people are exempt from immigration laws because they are descendants of Indigenous peoples.[36] Certainly Central and South America have Indigenous people who occupied the lands and territories long before foreign settlers made contact, but to simply infer that Indigenous people from another nation inherently hold right to occupy North America lands is concerning. If Indigenous people from another nation/country hold inherent rights to American land just because they're Indigenous per se, then this concept could easily justify European settlements as the white Europeans could argue that they too are Indigenous to their own European lands. Now everyone knows how ludicrous an argument like that would be to suggest that ethnic Germans, British, Irish or French might hold a right of claim to North American lands due to the fact that they are Indigenous to their own European lands. Indeed there are many Indigenous people in Central and South America, but they are Indigenous to their own ancestral lands and not the lands of other Indigenous peoples. Simply because they are Indigenous to their own lands south of the border shouldn't give them an inherent right to claim land in another country such as America. The Europeans are

---

[35] http://www.british-israel.ca/America.htm#.XFy5uYxE2hA

[36] https://www.foxnews.com/politics/ocasio-cortez-calls-to-abolish-ice-says-latinos-must-be-exempt-from-immigration-laws-because-they-are-native-to-us

not Indigenous to Canada –as they were to Europe –just as the South American peoples are not Indigenous to North America –as they are to South America. Suggesting that Indigenous people from another country should be able to claim land in a different country they aren't Indigenous to would be absolutely ludicrous. But when you examine how generous contemporary immigration programs and policies are in Canada, especially through multiculturalism, it might be very possible to justify the argument that non-Indigenous people do indeed have a claim to settle in Canada.

Indigenous peoples opposing multiculturalism

Giving credence to the concept that Indigenous people and immigrants can occupy colonized lands together and that simply because the immigrants are non-white and benefit from government a mandated program of multiculturalism is certainly a pondering thought. The apparent approval of non-white immigrants having a social alliance with Indigenous people can be deduced from the fact that there is no major dissenting voice or overt disapproval of multiculturalism from the Indigenous community itself. It would be expected that dissenting voices to contemporary immigration would be justified considering how European colonialism negatively impacted the traditional way of life for the Indigenous people. The same disdain should be expected for multiculturalism – that encompasses a wide variety of immigration methods such as refugee intakes, family reunification, student visas, work visas or any other method of immigration – which all amount to an open border concept resulting in millions of new settlers coming to Canada in recent decades. Despite how multiculturalism is essentially a covert word for open borders, there is little dissent to contemporary immigration from the Indigenous community in Canada. There was however one notable circumstance where a Canadian politician and former National Chief of the Assembly of First Nations expressed contempt against immigration in Canada.

David Ahenakew was an Indigenous man from Saskatchewan who stated that he believed that Jews were a disease in Germany and that Hitler was trying to clean them up. This was after he made reference to "goddamn immigrants" in Canada. Ahenakew recalled how some German people had told him that he was blessed to be Indigenous, but that that blessing was being destroyed by immigrants, specifically the Jews.[37] David Ahenakew came under a great deal of fire from the mainstream media and the Canadian Jewish community for his viewpoints relating to immigration resulting in charges of promoting hatred and the revocation of his

---

[37] https://en.wikipedia.org/wiki/David_Ahenakew

Order of Canada. After lengthy court proceedings and appeals, Ahenakew was found not guilty in 2009.[38] Despite the controversy that Ahenakew fuelled, he was regarded as an advocate for Aboriginal rights and education in Canada where he helped establish the Saskatchewan Indian Cultural College and the the First Nations University of Canada.[39] It can only be speculated at this point if Ahenakew had genuine hatred for immigrants or Jews but he certainly had a passion and drive to help his people move forward in a white settler-society that prides itself as a multicultural country of immigrants and celebrates diversity through strength.

• • • • • • • • • • • • • •

Canada's focus on mass immigration, and calling it multiculturalism, only serves to be an open border policy aimed at creating a national identity that doesn't reflect any Indigenous hereditament whatsoever. Canadian Obert Madondo is an immigrant from Zimbabwe who believes that he and other immigrants are treated respectfully and revered more than Canada's Indigenous people. Citing the fact that many Indigenous people live on reserves that are lacking in basic human needs such as access to water, heat, shelter, education etc., Madondo strongly contends that Canada has more of a focus on helping refugees than Indigenous people. Manondo stresses that Indigenous women are far more likely to endure violence than non-Indigenous women and that *racial caste* is alive and well and that Indigenous people bare the brunt of it. Madondo is extremely grateful for how Canada has treated him and is very thankful for the opportunity Canada provides him and many other refugees and immigrants. He is however perplexed at how Canada is the only western country where there are so many people from one racialize group (the Indigenous people) either missing or murdered.[40] Just like Madndo, millions of immigrants feel thankful to become citizens and for the opportunity that Canada has provided to them through the government mandated immigration programs that have been a part of official Canadian policies since its early inception as a white settler nation.

Chapter 5: Does Canada owe the world?

> When Canada accepts its immigrants, it often accepts the best ones from the selection therefore essentially taking the best people from a impecunious country.

[38] https://www.cbc.ca/news/canada/saskatchewan/judge-finds-ahenakew-not-guilty-in-2nd-hate-trial-1.802574
[39] https://www.thecanadianencyclopedia.ca/en/article/david-ahenakew
[40] https://www.huffingtonpost.ca/obert-madondo/missing-and-murdered-first-nations-women_b_1936308.html

As multiculturalism takes hold in Canada, it becomes apparent that people question whether or not the program is actually as beneficial as politicians and open border advocates say it is. A common theme is that Canada has a duty to help the world by tackling global issues such as poverty, war displacement, human rights violations, environmental matters and global health, just to name a few [41], and that Canada must use its immigration programs to do so to address these issues. This is a very noble gesture considering that Canada is a first world country that holds a great deal of wealth from natural resources and wealth in the form of individual and corporate financial capital. Despite the fact that Canada is widely active in bestowing financial aid to many countries that are not as privileged to have the resources that Canada does, there is still the conception that immigration into Canada will somehow solve world poverty. Immigration is however used as a political tool to create an appearance that Canada is a compassionate nation because people from impoverished countries can achieve the Canadian dream and the government is there to help them do so. Politicians are more than willing to sell an idea that Canadians are privileged and that sharing this privilege is an obligation because it's the Canadian way. Canada spends billions of dollars on foreign aid and politicians want that number increased significantly.[42] The aid that Canada generously gifts to poorer nations is used to build schools, hospitals and infrastructure and to develop clean water programs and agricultural projects just to name a few.

The Organization for Economic Co-operation and Development is the government body that ensures foreign aid is distributed accordingly and ensures that it reaches the people it's intended to. The OECD has a mandate to ensure that Canada is represented as a compassionate nation who wishes to spread its wealth to the needy of the world. Canada is indeed a very wealthy nation and Canadians are among the most generous people on earth and Canada certainly sets an example of how wealthy nations should assist in managing and eliminating world poverty. The OECD is simply a government extension of the generosity of Canadians and it can't be disputed that the organization does tremendous work worldwide.

Despite how Canada gives billions of dollars to impoverished countries through this organization, there is still a call from politicians demanding that Canada open

---

[41] https://www.international.gc.ca/world-monde/issues_development-enjeux_developpement/index.aspx?lang=eng

[42] https://www.oecd.org/newsroom/canada-needs-to-increase-foreign-aid-flows-in-line-with-its-renewed-engagement.htm

the doors of immigration to the financially destitute of the world. This means that Canada should be compelled to accept immigrants who are suffering from poverty as a duty to help eliminate world poverty. The fact that uprooting and displacing a desperately poor person and bringing them into Canada is somehow going to put a dent in world poverty is merely a political smoke and mirror performance. When Canada accepts its immigrants, it often accepts the best ones from the selection therefore essentially taking the best people from an impecunious country. This basically serves as an injustice to the country that the immigrants come from because now Canada has just stolen an able bodied person that could be used to help build/ develop their own country; with the assistance of the OEDC and the foreign aid of course. Accepting the best and the brightest immigrants is a benefit for Canada, but a clear disadvantage for the country who just lost a skilled person thus defeating the purpose of helping a disadvantaged country develop.[43] There is no doubt that Canada is an extremely generous country, and it is especially generous when it comes to issues of disadvantaged women and girls. Prime Minister Justin Trudeau was very benignant when he announced on Twitter that he'd give 50 million dollars to celebrity Trevor Noah who was raising money for Education Cannot Wait, a charity that helps girls gain access to schooling.[44] Although Trudeau was criticized for the method in which he donated the money, it still demonstrates the power an elected Prime Minister has to control tax payers money in the name of social justice and the attempt at tackling world poverty.

If Trudeau wanted to pledge the money he could have simply done it through a number of bureaucratic avenues, but instead he chose a popular venue that featured a well known celebrity and used social media to do so. Justin Trudeau also came under criticism when he gave 50 million dollars to the United Nations Palestinian refugee agency, which the United States has declared to be morally flawed due to its alleged connections to Hamas. Trudeau justified his actions by claiming it would assist with health care and education needs for Palestinian refugees – mainly women and girls who were caught up in the conflict in the disputed Arab and Israeli regions.[45] Again, this demonstrates how a Canadian politician can be extremely generous with tax payer's money in the name of helping other people around the world. With the billions of dollars in foreign aid allotted in the federal budget and arbitrary monetary gifts in the millions from the Prime Minister, it could therefore only be prudent that that Canada shouldn't need to take in

---

[43] https://youtu.be/LPjzfGChGlE

[44] https://www.ctvnews.ca/politics/trudeau-criticized-for-tweet-to-trevor-noah-pledging-50m-charity-gift-1.4202127

[45] https://www.ctvnews.ca/politics/canada-gives-50m-to-un-palestinian-refugee-agency-that-u-s-says-is-flawed-1.4131874

immigrants under the conception that it will help reduce world poverty. But Canada does have a political mandate to help the worlds impoverished and one way it does this is through refugee intake and family reunification, which is then celebrated as one of the many tiers of multiculturalism.

Family reunification

Canada's very generous immigration program is also extended to family members of immigrants who are already settled in Canada. Family reunification allows immigrants to sponsor their spouses, parents, grandparents, children and siblings. The program is very generous and it is an attractive reason why many immigrants choose Canada as a place to migrate to. The fact Canada also has very lavish social programs that include health care, education, old age security and much more is a real incentive for someone who is making a choice as to which country they should settle in. It's a far cry from the days of early European settlers who didn't have any social safety net whatsoever to rely on if things went sideways. In today's society, the government virtually assumes a great deal of responsibility for new settlers by either funding direct programs, such as the ones mentioned, plus programs that help with language, finding employment and many more indirect programs through non-government organizations. Indirect programs through non-government organizations are often funded by the government include ones that offer employment counselling and placement and assists immigrants with finding housing. This is certainly not what early European settlers had in order to make them comfortable and ensure that they would feel a sense of national unity despite the fact that the colonial powers allowed them to access Indigenous lands and resources for survival. Family is definitely an element that also helps new immigrants feel a sense of national unity and it's also an incentive for immigrants to lobby politicians. Politicians are more than glad to oblige and appease the masses of immigrants who claim that they need their family to ensure their settlement is successful and in order to be an integral part of mainstream Canadian society.

· · · · · · · · · · · · · ·

The Trudeau government has eliminated the previous governments lottery scheme that was used for accepting the family of immigrants. The Liberals have however proudly announced that they will take in over 20 thousand family members of immigrants that are already settled here through a mass reuniting process that is being hailed as a humanitarian achievement. Immigration Minister Ahmed Hussen is capitalizing off this political gesture that will add even more to the multicultural composition of Canadian society.[46] The political capital to be gained is why there is minimal objection from the political opposition, such as the Conservatives, who realize that this political capital that is gained from showing compassion toward the parents and grandparent of new settlers can certainly be beneficial politically. Minister Ahmed Hussen is definitely attempting to gain every possible political edge that he can by showing compassion to cultural minorities and by accepting large numbers of new settlers into a multicultural Canada. In a series of boastful tweets on Twitter, Hussen ensured that his stance on family reunification is well known and that he had to fix a problem that the previous Conservative government had caused.[47]

The family reunification program certainly sounds like a benevolent feature of a multicultural society that mandates inclusiveness, equality and the protection and freedom to ensure that someone's culture is cherished as part of the national identity and enshrined as a civil right. This protected-enshrined right to maintain one's culture as a feature of Canadian identity and inclusiveness is driven by politicians who maintain that it's the best thing for a productive Canada. Colonialism that encouraged white European settlers to immigrate to Canada held the same notion: a notion that foreigners being injected into Indigenous lands was the best course of action in order to create a great nation and to benefit the Indigenous people with European technology. When modern day politicians – just like colonial European leaders of the past – maximize a notion that they know what's best for the development of a nation by implementing policies that can impact Indigenous people and their lands, it's merely a demonstration of political currency used to gratify the colonizers. Of course the politicians of past and present claim that they know how to develop a nation by selling a notion or concept through the guise of legislating what's best for the nation and suggesting that any opposition to it is anti-Canadian. The political exploits by Minister Ahmed Hussen – by selling the concept of open borders to Canadians and phrasing it at as family reunification – allows him to acquire valuable political currency that he can use to appear as a champion of the underprivileged despite the fact he is doing it on the backs of the Indigenous people who have already suffered from past colonialism.

Refugee intake on a large scale

---

[46] https://www.cbc.ca/news/politics/lottery-immigration-reunification-1.4791705
[47] https://mobile.twitter.com/HonAhmedHussen/status/1075111584765263873

Immigration Minister Ahmed Hussen is also an advocate for refugee intakes at a scale not seen before in Canadian history. Canada is a very compassionate nation and Canadians are perhaps the most generous people in the world, especially when it comes to helping the impoverished. Refugees are however the politicians pride and joy and Hussen is promoting it beyond what any Canadian politician has ever done historically. Promoting this large scale form of immigration allows politicians like Hussen to acquire political capital by promoting Canada as a compassionate nation that will offer refugees an opportunity of a lifetime in an all inclusive nation that will accommodate their needs. Canada has agreed to be a signatory to a United Nations non-binding agreement whereby migrants who wish to seek asylum in Canada can do so from anywhere in the world and Canada must agree to take them as asylum seekers. The UN is infamous for making its demands obligatory on member states and advocating open borders; especially open borders of first world white settler nations such as Canada.[48]

Political currency is therefore gained by politicians while benefiting a political cause that is deemed to be in the best interest of all Canadians and the national identity of a country built by immigration. Any opposition to it only results in accusations of racism, xenophobia and or bigotry and that's certainly not what any politician wants; especially politicians who wish to gain political currency. The irony to this is that the vast majority of voters will not express their distain about dysfunctional immigration programs or openly vote for or support a political candidate or party that opposes unnecessary immigration. The idea that opposition to immigration is racist is exactly inline with the notion that white European colonialism was racist because it flooded Indigenous lands with non-Indigenous people therefore displacing the Indigenous people. European colonialism is evidently a form of racism due to the influx of a Eurocentric culture, language and the expectation of white values that have stripped and continue to prevent any advancement of Indigenous culture.[49] Many critical race theorists concur that this statement is true and that it was indeed the influx of white Eurocentrism that utterly destroyed the Indigenous people of Canada and that it was racially motivated due to the conception that European colonialism was superior to any Indigenous way of life. The fact that Canada is accepting immigrants in this unconventional way, when compared to past European colonialism, seems to be justified as it doesn't resemble the white immigration that stole land and natural resources from the Indigenous people centuries ago despite the fact that there will

---

[48] https://www.theglobeandmail.com/politics/article-un-asks-canada-to-resettle-more-refugees-displaced-in-horn-of-africa/

[49] http://www.icscollaborative.com/webinars/critical-race-theory-and-its-implication-for-indigenous-cultural-safety

be even more of a demand for land and resources through multiculturalism. It also appears rather hypocritical for Canada to demand that citizens of foreign countries be treated according to Canadian human rights standards – despite the kindness behind the demand – when there are imminent issue relating to Indigenous women and girls who have experienced what is described as a genocide against them.

Burnco Gelinas-Faucher a University of Montreal international law expert believes that Canada's attempt to be a party to an international genocide lawsuit against Myanmar sends the wrong message to Canada's Indigenous people. After the national inquiry into murdered and missing Indigenous women and girls concluded that Canada's Indigenous people are victims of a genocide, defending Rohingya Muslims as victims of a genocide and fighting on their behalf can be perceived as contradiction on the part of the Canadian government.[50] Due to the political nature of multiculturalism that makes Canada a global country and obligating it to offer refugees a new life in Canada, multiculturalism now creates an obligation to be a signatory to such an international lawsuit despite how it ignores a genocide at home involving its own Indigenous people. Countries that aren't multicultural and who are mono-ethnic don't participate in such international programs or in offering relocation, assistance and citizenship to those suffering genocide outside of their country therefore placing the onus on Canada to do so because of its official declaration of being multicultural.

If Canada is a nation of immigrants then colonialism must have been successful: right?

Canada's population stands at just over 37 million and has seen an increase of just over one million since Justin Trudeau took office. Politicians and immigrant advocates rejoice at these numbers and claim that they are just the beginning of a major boost in population that they claim Canada desperately needs. One immigrant advocacy group, the Century Initiative, wants to see the Canadian population at 100 million by the year 2100, and to do that, the group suggests that Canada take in at least 450,000 immigrants a year instead of the current 310,000.[51] The group claims that Canada will need at least this many immigrants in order to fill labour shortages and to ensure that Canada is economically competitive on the world scale. Politicians are setting the stage for the immigration increase which

---

[50] Indigenous genocide finding hangs over Canada's Myanmar court intervention
Cries of the pot calling the kettle black are emerging after Canada joined an international genocide lawsuit against Myanmar, because the national inquiry into missing and murdered Indigenous women and girls said Canada's Indigenous Peoples are genocide victims.
[51] http://www.centuryinitiative.ca/

will see the yearly number increase to 350,000 people by 2021. Minister Ahmed Hussen wants the 40,000 person increase as a means to address a severe labour shortage, ensure global competitiveness and to demonstrate how Canada is a welcoming country and a leader in attracting skills.[52] Likewise, Conservative politician Andrew Scheer also doesn't have any objections to mass immigration after he told Patrice Roy of Radio Canada that it's not about too much immigration it's about ensuring that there are services ready to welcome them.[53] The notion that Canada needs immigration to sustain itself as a country is a common theme among politicians and immigration supporters. It's a very difficult notion to refute without opening up the xenophobia and racism issue, even if refuted on genuine grounds rooted in logical arguments. The sentiment that immigration was necessary in order to develop the country was hailed as an integral and necessary part of European colonialism and was flaunted as an imperative means politically, economically and socially to ensure that new lands were efficiently conquered and developed. Bruce Gilley controversially stated this in his infamous academic article entitled *The Case for Colonialism* where he further suggests that a new program of colonialism is needed to control the functions of third world countries.[54] [55] Coincidentally enough, the same supporting sentiment can be found by merely listening to politicians, intellectuals and social justice advocates who all submit that immigration was and is a good thing simply because it was used to build a nation and it's still needed to ensure the maintenance of the nation and to build the nation further. So it's only prudent to say that praising past and present immigration as being a good thing would then logically suggest that colonialism itself must have been good despite how it used immigration as a conquering tool. To justify this sentiment the politicians, intellectuals and social justice advocates must focus on the element of diversity and racial equality by endorsing a mass immigration concept called multiculturalism. They can now believe that as a nation we are post colonial and that modern immigration is actually a positive thing that does no harm to Indigenous people, their lands and resources.

Is colonialism finished? Have we achieved post colonialism?

Colonialism, as it was centuries ago, does not exist today. There is no European monarchy in search of new worlds, new resources, new life, new opportunities to gain loyalists and new wealth. The fact that there is no current colonial power

---

[52] https://nationalpost.com/news/politics/canada-to-increase-annual-immigration-admissions-to-350000-by-2021

[53] https://twitter.com/PatriceRoyTJ/status/1087479399555813376?s=20

[54] Bruce Gilley (2017) The case for colonialism, Third World Quarterly, DOI: 10.1080/01436597.2017.1369037

[55] https://www.currentaffairs.org/2017/09/a-quick-reminder-of-why-colonialism-was-bad

taking over the unexplored regions of the world doesn't mean that there isn't powers that are still oppressing Canada's Indigenous people. To actually sit back and fail to consider the consequences of further immigration on the Indigenous people and fail to consider how it amounts to a contemporary form of colonialism is purely ignorant. The word *ignorant* is a strong pejorative, but it begs the question: why aren't people screaming that more immigration is still a form of colonialism even though it's not European? Moreover, why aren't Canada's Indigenous people screaming at the top of their lungs, "enough is enough"? There is complete silence from all the social justice warriors who advocate Indigenous rights and who proclaim that the colonial whiteness in contemporary Canadian society is still having detrimental effects on all Indigenous people.

Consequences stemming from generational victimization are said to be the current cause as to why Canada's Indigenous people severely lag behind in many social respects ranging from high suicide rates, proportionally higher school dropout rates, high incarceration rates, high poverty rates, high disease rates and high drug and alcohol rates. There has however been a number of academic studies and mainstream media stories relating to how the negative consequences of residential schools have perpetuated high rates of the mentioned social issues within Indigenous communities. Susan Pinker details how the uprooting of Indigenous children by the European colonial residential school system has literally changed the lives of generations of Indigenous people in an extremely negative way.[56] So it's not as if there isn't knowledge of the damage that European colonialism has had on Indigenous people, in fact there's collections of academic research, news reports and harrowing first hand stories that indicate the horrific damage that Indigenous people suffered at the hands of European colonialism. There is however a loud silence regarding how contemporary immigration could potentially create an entire new set of negative circumstances for Indigenous people.

· · · · · · · · · · · · · ·

No One Is Illegal (NOII)[57] is a social justice group that actually advocates open borders, mass immigration, multiculturalism and the elimination of colonialism and racism. Eliminating colonialism and racism is precisely what any social justice group would strive for in a white settler society, but the parallel concept of

---

[56] https://www.theglobeandmail.com/opinion/the-trauma-of-residential-schools-is-passed-down-through-the-generations/article24828005/
[57] https://noii-van.resist.ca/

advocating open borders at the same time seems somewhat ironic. It begs the question as to how a white settler society can begin to address the issues and effects of colonialism, which have severely hurt the Indigenous people, by even colonizing the lands further with more non-Indigenous people. The NOII has a mandate that places all people of colour in an oppressed category of persons who have suffered at the hands of colonialism, much the same as the Indigenous people have. They basically advocate that populating the already colonized lands with non-white/non-Indigenous people will somehow solve the problem and remedy the effects of European colonialism and racism. The fact that NOII are staunch advocates for open borders, mass refugee intakes and social diversity through multiculturalism is in conflict with the concept of how colonialism had a mandate of populating Indigenous lands with non-Indigenous people in the first place. The NOII also advocates against capitalism where they claim it creates oppression against people of colour as it exploits the natural resources of the lands and only serves to benefit the wealthy. The social justice advocacy of NOII is very extensive and delves into many areas of how a white settler society has numerous facets designed to specifically oppress all non-whites. They have several social causes that intersect racially, culturally and socially. I discovered this group back in 2010 when they were extremely vocal about the Vancouver Olympics after they claimed it was taking place on stolen land. Their claim sounds like an honourable argument considering that the government was essentially funding a colonial style project on Indigenous lands and that it took much needed money away from First Nations Peoples.

It's incongruous how they claim that Indigenous people are suffering at the hands of a colonial society that was specifically designed to advance white settlers through the immigration of non-Indigenous people. Advocating open borders, mass immigration and multiculturalism will certainly not help reconcile the previous damage that past colonial immigration inflicted on the Indigenous people. The social justice cause of defending Indigenous lands against a capitalistic and Eurocentric venture, such as the olympics, is something that would be expected from a principled group who holds bonafide concerns. The 2010 Olympic resistance movement in British Columbia was prevalent when many Indigenous people demanded that the government cease the undertaking of the Vancouver Olympics due to the fact that the lands were considered sacred and the money spent on such a venture was frivolous. This concept completely correlates with a social justice cause of how colonialism has created white structures within contemporary society that have adverse effects on Indigenous people. Using pristine mountainous landscapes for the olympics and spending millions of dollars on it is definitely a social cause that is worth fighting for if someone opposes

European colonialism. There couldn't perhaps be a better cause to oppose than an actual Eurocentric representation of whiteness, like the olympics, who has its historical roots in Greece and no connection to the Canadian Indigenous way of life whatsoever.[58] Opposing the 2010 Vancouver olympics as a direct protest to a contemporary colonial policy is what would be expected of Indigenous people who were victimized by colonialism. Yet when someone advocates that contemporary immigration is necessary in order to benefit the country and remedy the negative effects of European colonialism, it becomes clearly apparent that there's a conflict of ideology.

It appears that those who believe that contemporary immigration won't negatively effect the Indigenous people are also unconcerned about a past colonial system that used immigration to flood lands with settlers: European settlers who changed the face of Canada into a white settler society. So evidently more immigration shouldn't be the answer. Canada has however built entire governments that are based on the concept of contemporary immigration by citing how Canada is a country of immigrants thereby making it a modern day success. Along with these immigration based governments come huge bureaucracies and loads of taxpayers' money to support non-government organizations to assist newcomers. This is where the ideas of diversity, cultural enrichment and social tolerance are established and where governments begin dictating what's best for the social construction of a nation. As the governments pursue their immigration agenda that resembles centuries old European colonialism, there is always token gratitude given to Indigenous people by acknowledging that it's their land and thanking them for the privilege of occupying it. These kind acts of tokenism are only meant to distract Indigenous people away from the fact that contemporary immigration is merely a form of mass colonialism at a scale even larger than it was centuries ago. Instead, social justice advocates have a strong focus on how immigration is a net benefit for Canada and how it makes Canada a better place while failing to see how it's only a guise for the reincorporated immigration of non-Indigenous people. Reincorporated immigration now occurs under government mandated programs such as refugee intakes, poverty reduction immigration and family reunification and are all said to create strength through diversity and then called multiculturalism.

When compared to initial European colonialism centuries ago, there is no difference in the fact that a ruling governmental authority mandates the influx of non-Indigenous people into Indigenous lands. Initial European colonialism into

---

[58] http://vancouver.mediacoop.ca/olympics/olympic-resistance

Canada was alleged to be beneficial for the growth of the nation, good for the Indigenous people, good for the economy, good for humanity, good for society, etc. Modern day immigration is certainly a far cry from centuries old European colonialism, but it also rings true with the same cushy-feel-good kind of government program wherein only the government knows what's best for the common people to make the country a better place and if you oppose it you're unpatriotic. In the case of contemporary immigration that uses multiculturalism as its enforcer, opposition to it results in accusations of racism on top of being unpatriotic. This double edged sword is what keeps politicians and voters at bay and ensures that the government mandated program of multiculturalism continues in the same way that European colonialism did. While Indigenous people watch their land become further colonized by contemporary settlers, they can take small comfort in having social justice advocates proclaim that the government has a necessity to protect the Indigenous people and their lands, while at the same time, advocating mass immigration in the name of diversity. The nobility of those social justice warriors who advocate mass immigration is very shallow because they generate so much apathy within Indigenous communities who watch their lands become further colonized. Perhaps this is why there is no protest from the Indigenous people and demands that there be no more colonization of their lands and perhaps why there appears to be a collective sense of apathy and defeat.

Doug Cuthand is an Aboriginal writer who advocates for multiculturalism in order for Canada to move ahead socially. He contends that there is no reason for Indigenous people to fear cultural diversity so long as they aren't forced to change their religion or ways. Cuthand states that there are 35 million people in Canada and only one million are members of the original First Nations and that there shouldn't be an issue with more immigration. He is proud that Canada has made a home for diverse groups of people and believes that Canada should reflect more of the worlds population and be a place for immigrants to have a better life.[59] The embracing attitude of Cuthand – regarding immigration into land that is still deemed to be the land of Indigenous people stolen for the purposes of European colonialism – is obviously at odds with the protest against the 2010 Vancouver olympics. Indigenous people and social justice organizations staunchly opposed the 2010 olympics due to the claim that there would be negative effects on Native land and people.[60] The open border theory of Cuthand contradicts the theory that olympic games negatively impact Indigenous people and their culture. Opposition to a Eurocentric-capitalistic venture, such as the olympics, would be the most

---

[59] https://www.cbc.ca/news/indigenous/opinion-indigenous-perspective-on-immigration-1.4008365
[60] http://vancouver.mediacoop.ca/olympics/no-olympics-stolen-land/6314

expected response from social justice advocates who want to protect Indigenous people and land. Oil pipelines, golf courses, industrial parks and many other Eurocentric-capitalistic ventures are also vigorously opposed due to possible adverse effects on Indigenous people and lands. But there is no opposition to any Eurocentric-capitalistic ventures that involve the placement of non-Indigenous people into Indigenous lands regardless of the cost financially, culturally, socially or regardless of the need for new settlers to obtain housing or land, employment and the use of natural resources.

Chapter 6: Capitalism, renamed as multiculturalism, is a driving factor for politicians to encourage immigration

> *The elite immigrants can basically buy their way into Canada while the non-elite immigrants must beg their way in.*

Provincial nomination programs, known as PNPs, allow for immigration to Canada for the purpose of business development or to gain skilled or semi-skilled workers. The province or territory will specify what it needs relating to the type of immigrant and then assist in sponsoring them through the nomination program. There is usually a fee/deposit that the potential immigrant is required to pay and a set of conditions attached to the fee. If the immigrant agrees to set up a business or work as a skilled or semi-skilled worker, within a certain period of time, then the fee/deposit is refunded to them and they receive a permanent resident citizenship card. If the conditions are not met then the fee is forfeited to the province while the immigrant can still receive their permanent resident citizenship card.[61] Essentially the immigrant can still obtain permanent residency so long as they simply pay the fee/deposit to the province or territory due to the fact that the province or territory sponsors them. It's a system that is open for abuse from wealthy immigrants who want to purchase their citizenship by promising the sponsoring province or territory that they will participate in the economy. Wealthy immigrants can clearly afford to fork over the fee/deposit and then renege – even when the fee/deposit is in the hundreds if thousands of dollars. It's a very simple and efficient way for the wealthy to buy Canadian citizenship while still remaining citizens of their native country. The province or territory doesn't necessarily lose out due to the fact that they have now gained additional revenue through the fee/deposit. If the nominated immigrant does setup a business or provides a skilled labour then the province or territory has evidently gained in terms of business development. From this

---

[61] https://www.canada.ca/en/immigration-refugees-citizenship/services/immigrate-canada/provincial-nominees.html

perspective it can be argued that immigration is a net gain and a benefit for society by increasing the corporate tax base and by creating jobs. When comparing this type of immigration to asylum seekers or refugee claimants it goes to show that immigration can be divided into economic categories that specify elite and non-elite immigrants where the elite has money and the other doesn't. The elite immigrants can basically buy their way into Canada while the non-elite immigrants must beg their way in. Politicians can exploit both forms in order to achieve political gain. Allowing someone to pay their way in or beg their way in essentially creates a simplified system that amounts to an open border concept. Politicians can be revered for saving the economy or making the economy better when they enforce the purchasing of citizenship through PNP programs. Likewise, politicians can also be revered for saving humanity when they enforce taking in asylum seekers and refugees due to the fact that it is the humanitarian thing to do thus bolstering their political image.

Immigration nomination programs are driven mainly by the concept that immigration will help the economy by creating jobs, while asylum and refugee programs help increase the population of the unskilled workforce who can work unskilled jobs. Having a larger labour pool of unskilled workers keeps wages lower hence benefiting corporations by reducing their labour costs and increasing their profits. Politicians can gain corporate allies while claiming to save the impoverished by offering them a chance to work at minimum wage. Capitalism and open borders go hand and hand and politicians are the facilitators. Elite immigrants can buy their way in while non-elites walk across the unguarded sections of the Canadian border and are greeted with open arms by the RCMP and border services who act as baggage porters that are employed by the politicians and then become wards of the state.

Immigrants are needed because of a labour shortage

How many times have you heard that immigrants are needed to fill the labour shortage gap and to do the jobs that Canadians don't want to do? Well this is a cliché that is commonly spewed by open border advocates and social justice warriors who are just as quick to claim that foreign workers and workers of colour are, at the same time, being exploited by employers. This exploitation concept isn't new, it's actually an argument made by the infamous 99 percenters who oppose big corporations and the free market. Ironically enough it's the corporations that support mass immigration due to the simple economic fact that mass immigration increases the pool of potential workers and creates more people competing for the job, which essentially results in overall lower wages therefore decreasing corporate labour costs. Free market economics is generally a politically right leaning ideology, but many conservatives support mass immigration, although they won't usually refer to it as *open borders,* only espouse that immigrants are needed to fill an ever increasing labour gap. Ann Coulter mentions this concept several times throughout her book titled *Adios America: The left's plan to turn our country into a third world hellhole,* in which she describes the corporate-free market need for immigration as one that only benefits the wealthy corporations because it supplies them with cheap labour.

Corporate profits are sure to be higher so long as a large labour pool keeps possible unskilled workers accepting jobs at lower wages. Where this concept contradicts itself is when a country, such as Canada, essentially has open border policies and there are still massive labour shortages despite the open borders. This contradiction exposes itself after tens of thousands of illegal immigrants walked over the Roxham Road border from the United States into Canada[62] (at the behest of Prime Minister Trudeau) and a province like Prince Edward Island has farmers who claim that they can't find workers to fill the labour void. It would only stand to reason that if there were over 50 thousand illegal immigrants who trekked across the Canadian border from the United States in hopes of finding a better life then there certainly should not be a labour shortage in any unskilled sector whatsoever. The issue is that these illegal border crossers are being housed, fed, clothed, cared for medically and much more at the decorum of the government, hence the taxpayers' dime, and farmers in P.E.I. and elsewhere in Canada can't find enough workers. Tens of thousands of illegal border crossers who broke the law by entering the country unlawfully are now wards of the state and not even thought of as people who could be used to solve a labour problem.

The government is constantly pushing mass immigration on Canadians by proclaiming that there is a severe labour shortage in rural areas. Immigration minister Ahmed Hussen insists that small rural towns often have only one major employer and that this employer is desperate for workers and that this desperation is having ill effects on those businesses. Hussen believes that Canada needs a major boost in immigration in order to offset this human deficit and that immigration is the only way to solve this problem. Hussen describes these new immigrants as "settlers" who will benefit the economy and benefit the

---

demographics of rural communities.[63] Now try and explain to an open border advocate, who declares that Canada needs immigrants because there's a labour shortage, that the only benefactor of this mass immigration is the corporations who want cheap labour. I highly doubt that it'll go over very well and I'm absolutely positive that you'll be called the usual plethora of words implying bigot, racist, un-Canadian, xenophobe etc. Moreover, tell the next Indigenous person you encounter that Canada needs loads of more immigrants to fill the labour gap created by wealthy corporations who are a direct product of white European colonialism and see if the argument gets you sympathy.

Birth tourism

Birth tourism in Canada is a unique way for foreigners to gain citizenship by simply being present on Canadian soil when their baby is born. Pregnant women only need to be in Canada merely as visitors while they give birth at a Canadian hospital and their children will automatically be declared citizens. This essentially means that the mother will also be granted citizenship by default. The default position is one that is simply done on the premise that the mother can't be forced to leave the country when her visitor's visa expires because her baby is officially a Canadian citizen. It's considered cruel and unusual punishment to separate a mother and child on the grounds of citizenship alone as the child born in Canada needs its mother to care for them, even if the mother is not a Canadian citizen. It's a fast ticket into Canada when a non-citizen woman gives birth on Canadian soil and it has become a very popular method of gaining citizenship. Critics of this immigration method believe that it's unregulated and encourages abuse and that the government should implement measures that prevent and discourage birth tourism. Advocates of immigration hold differing views where they contend that the process is equitable and allows for children and their families to have a life in Canada, or at least the children can have the option of always being a Canadian even if their mother/parents return to to their home country. The second contention of immigration advocates is rather frivolous because the chances of a late term pregnant woman simply making a visit to Canada as a tourist is rather unusual. On top of this, most airlines will not allow late term pregnant women on their aircraft while Canadian immigration and customs officers will usually scrutinize a tourist whom they believe is pregnant and may give birth on Canadian soil. Nevertheless, birth tourism has become a cottage industry where there are travel agencies and people who will facilitate the process thereby allowing women to give birth in Canada and gain citizenship.[64] In Richmond British Columbia the birth tourism

---

[63] https://youtu.be/4ZZXLlO3wcY

rate has increased substantially where one in four births is that of a visiting international mother and likewise in Vancouver where two hospitals see 14 percent of births also from international mothers.[65]

Despite the fact that birth tourism is fundamentally immoral, amazingly enough it's not necessarily illegal. If a travel agency specializing in country specific tours – such as Canadian vacations – decides to target clients from specific countries where tourists want to potentially immigrate to Canada, then obviously the travel agency can turn a blind eye to issues relating to a woman client being pregnant. Turning the blind eye to a pregnant client is as simple as pretending not to ask, while at the same time, targeting such clientele. The travel agency is under no obligation to advise the proper methods of immigrating to Canada other than advising on the necessary visas that are required to visit. Visas are not required for all visitors to Canada, while the visitors who require visas can be given six month visas and even extensions if desired. So this basically makes birth tourism an attractive and easy way to gain instant access to citizenship without going through the bureaucratic hoops where it could take years to obtain citizenship the conventional way and this way they simply get to jump the queue. Canada is prime ground for the facilitating of birth tourism due to the ethnic diversity in many large cities where specific ethnic groups can be targeted for the practice. Richmond, British Columbia is a city with a thriving Chinese population and has become an appealing location for overseas Chinese nationals who wish to participate in the birth tourism process. With the help of local Chinese Canadians in Richmond B.C., Chinese nationals can gain access to places known as baby houses where they are housed and assisted throughout their pregnancy and then taken to local hospitals to give birth. There is of course a fee that these baby houses charge but the benefits to the foreign nationals is that their newborns become anchor babies essentially anchoring the mothers to Canada as citizens.[66] This of course is just another method of immigration for non-Indigenous people to occupy Indigenous lands and resources and the mainstream media and open border advocates completely ignore this element of contemporary colonialism. Ignoring this issue is easy because it falls under the guise of diversity as strength and is a far cry from the initial white-European colonialism practices of immigration that favoured majority whites.

---

[64] https://torontosun.com/opinion/editorials/editorial-birth-tourism-in-canada-needs-to-be-addressed

[65] Richmond, B.C. politicians push Ottawa to address birth tourism and stop 'passport mill'
One in four births taking place at Richmond Hospital involve an international mother, according to new statistics.

[66] https://nationalpost.com/news/canada/birth-tourism-is-legal-but-unscrupulous-practice-is-generating-political-opposition-and-mobilizing-vigilantes

The immigration of non-Indigenous people into Canada can take on many forms and is praised by advocates and politicians as an achievement towards diversity, which is intended to create a more racially equitable society. There is however a major disconnect between what is good for Canada and what is good for politics. The old expression that someone is always generous with someone else's money sings true when it comes to immigration in Canada and the Indigenous people. Politicians are always generous with someone else's land and resources, especially when it adds capitol to their political standing. Prime Minister Justin Trudeau believes that immigrants have more of a stake in Canada then do established long standing Canadians because "we" take it for granted.[67] Trudeau actually went as far as to boast that he is jealous of new immigrants because they have chosen Canada as their new country. These comments raise concerns as to how a politician can infer that a nation, in which they themselves are a settler in, is something that they can simply give away while stating that there's people that don't appreciate the country. These comments also suggest that the Prime Minister has complete and total contempt for the Indigenous people who have been established citizens thousands of years before European colonization: the very colonization that granted power to the non-Indigenous people so that they can simply give away the land and its resources as they so wish through their established governments. It doesn't matter whether or not it's a controlled system of immigration, family reunification, a legislated multicultural program, a humanitarian refugee intake program or simply an immigration process that allows people to easily become Canadians, it's all a concept of open borders and an attempt to further colonize Indigenous lands thus amounting to contemporary colonialism.

Saying that Canada needs immigrants is like saying that Canada needed colonialism

By introducing large amount of non-Indigenous/non-white immigrants into Canadian society, advocates of multiculturalism can now use concepts like *strength through diversity* as a foundation for their argument. In other words, multiculturalists will use any method of immigration to suggest that the concept of diversity is a tool that can reduce the effects of colonialism and the white settler society therefore creating racial equality. Multiculturalism is essentially a broad term that can be interchangeable with immigration, open borders, refugee intakes and unfettered mass immigration in general. All these terms are the terms used by the multiculturalists in order to advance their agenda of implementing contemporary colonialism. Straight immigration that is not related to the ideology

---

[67] https://globalnews.ca/news/3567893/justin-trudeau-jealous-immigrants-ctv-interview/

of multiculturalism entails the process of people immigrating to Canada for a variety of reasons. Politicians claim that immigration is necessary for Canadian society because the national birth rate is low and there is a major labour shortage. Yes it's true that many Canadians born in Canada are choosing to have smaller families with an average birth rate of less than two children per family.[68] Politicians believe that this might present a future problem when there are more older adults who require care and social-security and not enough younger adults in the workforce paying into the country's tax base. There is also the issue that many older adults are getting ready to retire and that there won't be enough younger ones to fill the occupational void left by retirees. Finally there is the current labour shortage in many non-skilled fields such as fast food, farming and transportation. These reasons are why politicians claim that Canada needs immigrants and the reason why many voters also support this claim. It's certainly true that today's families are smaller than families of generations past and the foreseeable consequences could easily be inferred that there will be limited or no old-age-pension or social-security available for senior citizens due to fiscal shortages.

It's also very possible that if governments are faced with this dilemma then there will be no choice but to spread the cost out over the remaining taxpayers through tax increases. So yes there could be an argument made for immigration that would help off-set a deficiency of a low birth rate, but it would have to be manageable immigration and this is where governments fall short. Immigration on the manageable level is virtually non-existent in Canada and is instead replaced by multiculturalism that perpetuates mass immigration directly correlating with European colonialism of the past.

The fact that European colonial powers were the white man's imperial agenda that would redefine a nation and strip Indigenous people of their heritage should be no surprise to contemporary multiculturalists. But if you confronted a contemporary multiculturalists and suggested that their ideology is another form of colonialism – the same as past European colonialism that was government mandated – and accused them of implementing an imperialist agenda you'd probably be attacked. Attacked physically perhaps, but guaranteed you'd be called a racist, bigot, xenophobic, Islamophobic, nazi, etc. But what would happen if you directly compared the modern government mandated multiculturalism to European colonialism of the past and hypothesized that it's simply an imperialistic method of redefining a country? In this day and age of worshiping diversity, mass immigration and open borders, the concept of how multiculturalism harms

---

[68] https://www150.statcan.gc.ca/n1/pub/11-630-x/11-630-x2014002-eng.htm

Canada's Indigenous people is uncharted territory, politically and academically. Ironically enough, the very same multiculturalists would definitely support sovereignty for Indigenous people and the return of stolen land, while at the same time, failing to address the issue of how contemporary immigration would amount to a revival of colonialism by requiring even more lands and resources for the new settlers. Multiculturalism has all the hallmarks of initial European colonialism: influx of non-Indigenous into Indigenous lands, it's perpetrated by the white man, it's controlled and enforced by the government, it's intended on making society better for everyone and it's supported by the vast majority of citizens. This is what a *postnational* society looks like: it's called *diversity* and it's what every politician is selling through the concept of multiculturalism and the foundation of it is large scale immigration.

Chapter 7: Postnational-Canadian-values, but no core identity! Getting lost in diversity the post-colonial way.

> *This bond would somehow bring about a utopian product that would make Canada unique. The product would be one where there is no focus on nationalism, because nationalism might be considered the core root of contemporary racism in a white settler society.*

In 2015 after Prime Minister Justin Trudeau took office he stated that: There is no core identity, no mainstream in Canada....[There are shared values — openness, respect, compassion, willingness to work hard, to be there for each other, to search for equality and justice. Those qualities are what make us the first postnational state.][69] A postnational society can be considered a sell out to globalism and a defiance to nationalism. This is exactly what Trudeau wishes to promote when he champions diversity as strength. It's apparent that he believes that the only way to have different cultures live in harmony is to promote a concept where diversity somehow creates a social bond between different religious, ethnic and cultural groups of people. This bond would somehow bring about a utopian product that would make Canada unique. The product would be one where there is no focus on nationalism, because nationalism might be considered the core root of contemporary racism in a white settler society that was founded off the roots of European colonialism. This is a feasible concept when you view the country through a lens of race and how many policies of European colonialism wreaked

---

[69] https://en.m.wikipedia.org/wiki/Canadian_values

havoc on the Indigenous people, Blacks, Chinese and other non-European groups. Indeed European colonial policies demonstrated what we would deem today as pure-unadulterated racism, bigotry and hatred. But you would be hard pressed to find any remaining policies that purposely oppress non-whites. If there's one thing that Trudeau forgot to mention in his acceptance speech is the progress that Canada has made in terms of past colonial policies and how Canada is a world leader in equality and amelioration. In fact you'd also be hard pressed to name another country where Canadian citizens would rather immigrate to, instead it's people wanting to come to Canada as opposed to people wanting to leave Canada. This is obviously because of the social and political progress making Canada a world leader in racial equality.

Instead there's a focus on how Canada can be a global player by surrendering its national identity that reflects European colonialism and all the whiteness it represents. Making reference to the monarchy as part of Canada's history is taboo and an issue that politicians tippy toe around other than rare mentions of it. Canadian values do however go far beyond ignoring European colonialism and the devastation it had on the Indigenous people. Former Liberal Party leader Michael Ignatieff suggests that Canadian values are actually rooted in historical loyalty to the Crown.[70] The same contention was expressed by the Conservative Party of Canada in 2009 when they likewise suggested a similar sentiment. The fact that Canada still has a major connection to the Crown shouldn't be dismissed as negligent considering the social progress that has been made over the last several decades and the last century for that matter. Canadian values go far beyond what Justin Trudeau personally thinks is a result of nationalism. According to a University of Waterloo study, Canadians believe that fairness, inclusion, economic security, diversity, health, democracy, equity, safety and sustainability are all integral factors in defining what constitutes values in Canada.[71] None of these values suggest that Canada should erase it's European colonial past or suggest that Canada shouldn't have national pride. All of these Canadian values put forth in this study are actually derived from an open and tolerant culture that is very unique to Canada despite a dark racial history. It is essentially the Eurocentric colonial model of common law that allowed for the evolution of social progress leading to change that encourages and mandates equality. The collective values of all Canadians over the last century that have metamorphosed into an ideology of social equality where we see that diversity isn't the main pillar of strength: instead, it's the people themselves who are the main pillars of strength. It's the individual who recognizes

---

[70] D. Michael Jackson (2013). The Crown and Canadian Federalism. Dundurn. pp. 18–19.

[71] https://uwaterloo.ca/canadian-index-wellbeing/about-canadian-index-wellbeing/reflecting-canadian-values

that people's differences are not a barrier to achievement, but are a product of the evolution of democracy: the democracy that evolved from European colonialism and not a politically enforced concept aimed at erasing the past. But multiculturalism is a new version of mass immigration and it needs to be aligned with a cause that is contemporary in nature. Perhaps that's why politicians try and slide around this obvious connection between past immigration policies and contemporary immigration policies by claiming that it's *post nationalism* making it sound all legitimate and noble.

Diversity as strength is a multicultural phenomenon

Canada makes a strong effort in promoting a global image as one that is achieved through *diversity*. Multiculturalism uses the concept of diversity, which is engineered by the government who then instigates the ideology that Canada is *postnational*. The government can now justify their large scale immigration policies as being a major component of a doctrine that is an integral part of a national identity: a national identity that is moving towards post-colonialism and reconciliation with Indigenous people. But how can diversity through immigration amount to reconciliation or a post-colonial state? Unfortunately it's left up to a government that operates under an inherently engrained colonial white system to dictate what is defined as reconciliation and post-colonialism. As a result of this government intervention reeking of white colonial ways, there is an inclination to sell the idea that more immigration will somehow mend past wrongs and if you oppose it you're accused of being racist and of forgetting Canada's historical routes of how immigration built the nation.

Cultural enrichment through immigration

How often have you heard the phrase *cultural enrichment* and how great it is for a white settler society? I bet you've heard it quite a few times, and I bet you've heard it mostly from politicians, mainstream media types and big businesses. Cultural enrichment is the modern day buzzword that rings with jubilation and an enthusiastic echo that resonates with racial equality. There however is a great dilemma when opting to use this word within the context of implying that its connotation is somehow good for racial equality. Unambiguously suggesting that a community, city, province, state or country will need to be culturally enriched by solely embracing multiculturalism is as oxymoronic as assuming that the moon is made of cheese. The entire concept of cultural enrichment only implies to white settler countries and not to monoethnic or religious theocratic countries.

White settler countries, such as Canada, have become a prime example of how cultural enrichment can be enforced on society through government mandated programs, policies and legislation. Monoethnic and theocratic countries don't participate in cultural enrichment by way of multiculturalism or any other method of government forced cultural or immigration programs. Instead, many monoethnic and theocratic countries use the concept of immigration to their benefit in ways relating mostly to unskilled or undesirable labour or skill trades or professions. Unskilled or undesirable labour can consist of arduous work and or work that is considered peasantry in nature and only performed by those of low intellect. Skilled labour and professions, on the other hand, consists of work where there is a necessity for the work in order to advance society as a whole. Teachers, doctors and engineers are often cited as people who are needed to fill a gap in a structured social system and to train the etho-native population on the skills of the profession. In both cases of skilled and unskilled immigration, the monoethnic and theocratic countries will seldom retain the foreign worker when the necessity of their work expires.

Canada uses many aspects of so-called *necessary immigration* where immigrants are utilized to perform unskilled and skilled work, but they are not usually required to leave the country when the need for the work is fulfilled as they have several options at staking a claim to citizenship. Canada uses the ideology of foreign workers as a means of obtaining cheap labour for big businesses and for accessing professionals who have already been fully trained in another country and at the expense of their native country. Canada also loves to attract foreign students who attend professional programs such as medicine, dentistry and engineering because they pay a significantly higher tuition than domestic students. This is a great revenue generator for post-secondary institutions and a great way to cash in on the diversity bandwagon by promoting cultural enrichment.[72] Many foreign students also become permanent residents and citizens, while attending their studies, or shortly thereafter, thereby contributing their skills to society and becoming a constructive benefit. Having foreign students come to Canada is an all-around way for universities to foster diversity and advertise the social necessity of how important cultural enrichment is for racial harmony in society.

• • • • • • • • • • • • • • •

---

[72] https://cfs-fcee.ca/wp-content/uploads/2018/10/2015-05-Factsheet-IntUGrads-EN.pdf

Cultural enrichment, in its simplest form, comes by way of food. Yes food! Everyone in Canada enjoys the exotic meal at their local ethnic establishment thanks to massive immigration and official multiculturalism of course. Those wonderful exotic meals range from spicy to dicey and always ensure an unforgettable experience at a reasonable cost due to enormous competition. Every major city in Canada is full of exotic foreign restaurants and many more continue to open up everyday. I once spoke with a guy in Calgary who told me how appreciative he was of multiculturalism and how wonderful it was to delve into the Chinese culture and experience every aspect of it. He was bragging about the local Chinatown and all the cultural enrichment it offers. I was sort of baffled as to his excitement after he continued to insist that he never needs to travel anywhere due to the cultural diversity that Calgary offers. It seemed strange that he could be so content simply living in Calgary and not having any desire to travel anywhere else; especially internationally. Calgary is certainly a wonderful city that provides cultural enrichment due to its many festivals, restaurants and cultural enclaves, but I fail to see how that can be a replacement for experiencing the joys of visiting a foreign country in person and experiencing a culture first hand. This is what the cult of multiculturalism does to people, it persuades them into a narrow minded standpoint where they believe what the political elites do must be best for the common folk. At the same time, I also encountered people who openly welcomed multiculturalism while extending overt disdain towards Indigenous people. This contempt that worshipers of multiculturalism displayed towards the Indigenous people was often backed up with a sentiment of how they are non-tax paying people who are lazy and have no desire to be part of the Canadian society while immigrants from other countries want to be a diverse Canadian. Indeed many Indigenous people don't pay taxes when they live and work on reserves, but there are also large numbers of Indigenous people who do pay taxes and are occupationally active. As far as accusing Indigenous people of not wanting to be part of this so-called Canadian society that is luscious with cultural enrichment: Well who could blame them? Considering what colonialism did to them!

National hijab day is the Canadian way

Taking multiculturalism to the next level – whereas the definition of Canadian is construed as being diverse and post-colonial – is evident within the renowned celebration of the Islamic hijab. National hijab day is an informal celebration in many Canadian cities where multiculturalism is considered to be a defining factor. Encouraging women of all ages to sport the hijab in an act of multicultural solidarity is seen as something extremely Canadian and is celebrated in many countries.[73] Non-Muslim students at the University of Calgary demonstrated this solidarity with Muslim women by wearing a hijab during the university's celebration when students from the Muslim Student's Association (MSA) set up information booths. Non-Muslim students were schooled on the existence of Islamophobia in Canada and how the deadly Quebec mosque shooting was a prime example of that. The MSA assisted non-Muslim female students in the fitting process of the hijab and how it is normalized, not foreign, but actually empowering to women.[74] The aspect of normalized, not foreign and empowering, arises due to opposition to it after some Muslim women expressed discontent of the practice. Some Muslim women have claimed that the hijab is actually a symbol of oppression and male domination and that it has no basis in religious texts and is merely a cultural practice that is anti-Western.[75] Despite the opposition, the hijab has become a symbol of being Canadian and a statement of supporting social/religious/racial equality. Inferring that the hijab is un-Canadian and not conducive with Canadian society would most definitely result in accusations of racism, bigotry and especially Islamophobia, which is why most people simply capitulate, appease and then celebrate accordingly. Capitulating and appeasing is done under the guise of *celebrating* another's culture and showing tolerance as a good Canadian. National hijab day in Canada is therefore a contemporary social norm that defines what it is to be a Canadian and what it is to be post-colonial. But how does celebrating national hijab day in Canada benefit the Indigenous people and how does it define what Canada is and should be to them? Asking Indigenous people to celebrate such a pseudo holiday is like asking them to celebrate a white settler holiday and to expect them to accept it as cultural enrichment.

Alberta international education programs for k-12

Alberta has what it boasts as a unique program of study that allows students to embark on foreign language education as part of their school curriculum. Languages such as Spanish, Punjabi, Chinese, Arabic, Hebrew, Polish, German, Italian, Japanese and Ukrainian are all offered as a program of cultural enrichment or as a method for students to be accommodated in relation to their culture if need be. Bilingual programs such as these are designed to keep multiculturalism in mind and designed to capture the attention of immigrant Canadians. Capturing the attention of new immigrants serves as political capital whereas politicians can provide them with the feeling that they are an integral part of Canadian society while still keeping their language and culture. These bilingual programs are offered as part of the regular public school program and then integrated into various

---

[73] https://en.m.wikipedia.org/wiki/World_Hijab_Day

[74] https://globalnews.ca/news/3221075/non-muslims-in-calgary-show-support-by-wearing-a-hijab/

[75] https://www.gatestoneinstitute.org/7464/ottawa-hijab-day

schools according to demand.[76] Supporters of bilingual programs involving second languages that are not part of the official constitution believe it is a necessary aspect of multiculturalism because it allows the students to stay connected to their own native culture. The president of the Canadian Arab Friendship Association, Yazan Haymour, believes that bilingual education is a crucial step in achieving enrichment of linguistic and cultural diversity and allows better achievement on a social, academic and cultural level.[77] Alberta has embraced a Ukrainian immersion program due to the large number of Ukrainian settlers that made Alberta their home at the turn of the twentieth century. This immersion program is hailed as an achievement after the provincial government of the 1970's recognized a need to accommodate and preserve the Ukrainian culture which it believed was an integral part of the province's history.[78] Bilingual programs in Canada are not necessarily new, French immersion has been a popular choice for many parents who wish to have their children educated in both official languages. Public school systems across Canada provide bilingual education in French and English as a necessity to keep with the terms of the official constitution that specifies the two official languages of the country.

Private language schools have also offered many different language programs for those who wish to undergo continuing education or who wish to linguistically enhance their cultural language. In a country as ethnically diverse as Canada, it should be expected that there would be a demand of some sort for languages other than the official ones. Canada's Multiculturalism Act recognizes that there is a need to accommodate languages other than English and French and that these accommodations should be adhered to if possible. Besides this, it's never any harm to undertake the academic study of a different language for the purpose of enhancing ones own intellectual capacity. The issue or conflict begins to arise when consideration is given to the fact that foreign languages are being promoted either as a necessity or as a requirement to Canadian cultural inclusivity. When tax dollars are spent on the funding for foreign languages, which aren't traditional to Canada or specified in the constitution, conflict is surely to be inevitable. Indigenous people are losing their languages at record rates and there is a major struggle in Canada to regain such Indigenous languages. Certainly languages evolve and become instinct, but when there is a strong focus put on foreign languages as being a part of the Canadian identity this amounts to a slap in the face for Indigenous people who have all but lost their native languages.

---

[76] https://education.alberta.ca/international-languages-7-9/programs-of-study/

[77] https://www.ctvnews.ca/canada/alberta-to-offer-arabic-bilingual-program-across-province-next-fall-1.3626381

[78] https://www.kyivpost.com/ukraine-politics/ukrainian-bilingual-program-going-strong-in-canadas-alberta-province.html

Before colonization in Australia there were over 250 aboriginal languages, but today however there are barely 60 left.[79] This is a result of Christian missions that involved the schooling of Indigenous children by removing them from their homes in much the same manner as residential schools did in Canada. Colonial schooling of this nature forbid Indigenous children from speaking their native languages therefore creating a path of linguistic deterioration that is prevalent today in both Australia and Canada. The consequence of this linguistic deterioration has been the eradication of many Indigenous languages, which has indirectly and directly impacted their culture in negative ways. The loss of culture through loss of language is a major implication for Indigenous people because it drives them further away from mainstream society resulting in ghettoization. If multiculturalism is theoretically meant to bind society together by highlighting people's cultural and linguistic uniqueness then it clearly proves that ignoring and decimating Indigenous peoples' languages only reinforces the isolation element that colonialism was intended to achieve. This places undue pressure on Indigenous people to integrate into the colonial based society and accept their terms of multiculturalism and the recognition of non-indigenous languages. In Australia for example, many Indigenous people feel this pressure and believe that they must integrate into the white based society in order to achieve success and happiness. They feel that they must surrender what is left of their culture and history and capitulate to a system of whiteness.[80]

The government of Canada has however taken steps to preserve and advance what is left of the country's Indigenous languages through programs such as the Aboriginal Languages Initiative. The ALI has a mandate to preserve, resurrect and promote the development of Indigenous languages while providing an educational solution to address the loss of languages.[81] The revitalization of extinct Indigenous languages is a process that offers some reconciliation and amelioration for Indigenous people and the Canadian government has successfully capitalized on it. On top of promoting a multitude of foreign languages under the concept of diversity, the Canadian government has merely created a strategy where it attempts to show compassion for the ailing Indigenous languages as an act of tokenism. The grandiosity of the Canadian government to suggest that bilingualism in foreign languages are essential for strength through diversity and that foreign languages are essential to the existence of Canada – a as a globally competitive nation – is a prime example of contemporary colonialism.

---

[79] https://www.creativespirits.info/aboriginalculture/language/loss-of-aboriginal-languages
[80] https://www.abc.net.au/news/2016-08-27/aboriginal-people-pressured-to-lose-culture-study-says/7790928
[81] https://www.canada.ca/en/canadian-heritage/services/funding/aboriginal-peoples/languages.html

Indeed global corporations will require the talents of employees who speak foreign languages in order to advance their competitiveness and profitability, but how many corporations require employees who speak one of the hundreds of Indigenous languages that politicians are trying to preserve? The Canadian government's ALI program is celebrated as a solution to the loss of Indigenous languages and a step toward reconciliation by politicians who merely endorse it with money and praise in order to appear compassionate and to gain the attention of the voters. There has been in excess of 19 million dollars awarded toward the ALI initiative and over 80 million dollars allotted to the entire philosophy of revitalizing Indigenous languages in Canada in 2017.[82] Promoting this philosophy is political real estate for politicians who want to establish their territory within a special interest cause that appears to be compassionate towards a victimized and oppressed group of people.

Languages over poverty

The reality is that Canada's Indigenous people face grim circumstances due to poverty and this is a major contributing factor to social inequality. One in four Indigenous children on First Nations reserves live in poverty, suicide rates among Indigenous youth are 5 to 7 times higher than non-Indigenous youths and an Indigenous youth is more likely to end up in jail then graduate from high school.[83] So when politicians focus on addressing issues of lost and dying languages for Indigenous people, they simply only feed their own narcissism by using the issues to their own political advantage. Politicians offer money for programs that don't offer any concrete solutions towards reconciliation or amelioration as result of colonialism. Instead politicians have a major focus on providing bilingual training for non-official languages all in the name of racial equality and creating a diverse nation that is capable of competing on a global scale. This entire notion reeks of past colonialism whereas the colonial occupiers would use their legislative powers to make the acquired lands and resources available for their own use and the use of the colonial empire. Today the governmental powers make the same conquered lands diverse with non-Indigenous people who all have their cultural, linguistic and religious needs propitiated in order to gain votes and maintain political power.

Chapter 8: Accommodating multiculturalism as a social norm.

When examining the fact that it's fundamentally only white settler societies that implement and practice multiculturalism as official governing policies, the idea of reasonable accommodation becomes paramount.

[82]https:/ kina8ats- pports-

[83] https:/

A social norm can be used as a distinct term implying that there are social normalities within a white settler society that have a major influence on the culture and societal structure. Considering that most western nations are European colonial based, it should be mentioned that the term social norm will inevitably contain white based features and characteristics that can be considered the core identity of a white settler society. This concept would then dictate that whiteness plays a pivotal role in defining what the social structure of a white settler society is and how that social structure defines the cultural traditions expected as a social norm. White settler societies obviously have many social norms that would reflect the Eurocentric concepts of whiteness and these white based social concepts could hinder how multiculturalism is shaped. When examining the fact that it's fundamentally only white settler societies that implement and practice multiculturalism as official governing policies, the idea of reasonable accommodation becomes paramount. This implementation and practice of multiculturalism has had major influences on how European based social norms have become taboo and any attempt to endorse such European based social norms can be deemed as supporting a white ethnocentric perspective or just plainly racist. Social norm, as a term, now becomes the foundation for prescribing a set of *societal standards* where the interests and rights of collective groups take precedent over individual interests and individual rights. Setting these *societal standards* is achieved under the proposition where whiteness is a supposition that white settler societies are inherently an agency of oppression due to their Eurocentric social norms that facilitate racism. Non-white individuals, within a European based white settler society, are now intrinsically excluded from the mainstream cultural elements therefore making them victims of oppression by the white colonial powers. This makes the concept of individual rights appear applicable to only persons of a racially privileged group: the white European class who govern, make laws and set the social norms and cultural standards. Non-white individuals can now feel excluded as functioning members of a society that boasts equal rights, inclusiveness and equality; especially when those individuals are culturally different from the colonial based standards. The requirement of cultural differences from the mainstream colonial society may be in the necessity to wear certain religious clothing that conflicts with the social norms of a white based society.

The collective ideology of multiculturalism and the apparent victims

Reasonable accommodation is intended to be an equitable method of approaching a social situation where an individual has a special need that society should satisfy in the name of equality. This reasonable accommodation can encompass a broad and diverse entreaty making the need seem rather insignificant or even making it appear to be a *special* accommodation as opposed to a *reasonable* one. Cultural and religious needs are perhaps the most common accommodations that are petitioned, but special needs relating to disability may also produce a request of a reasonable accommodation. Cultural and religious needs may require a special accommodation that could include the requirement of an organization, group or business to adhere to a demand whereby there are exempt from certain conditions or must likewise be obligated to adhere to certain conditions. Exemptions from something could include being excused from complying with policies, regulations, legislations or laws while an obligation to something could be satisfying a cultural or religious need despite such policies, regulations, legislations or laws that specify otherwise. Common cultural and religious accommodations include compelling non-adherents to adopt to certain conditions that could involve granting the wearing of clothing, granting special prayer times or implementing gender segregation. Gender segregation, as a reasonable accommodation, can be requested when the white Eurocentric norms of how men and women share certain public spaces is challenged due to religious reasons. This is a situation where accommodating religious rights as a guarantee of social equality can create a conflict between how a white settler society is socially progressive in terms of how men and women are considered equal when in public. Reasonably accommodating the ultra conservative beliefs of Islam can however demand that the equality standards of a progressive white settler society like Canada be altered in the name of social equality. The University of Regina allowed special swim times in their public swimming pool that separated males from females in order to accommodate such ultra conservative religious beliefs. The university stood firm on their stance in doing so in order that the swimmers could learn basic swimming skills that were deemed to be lifesaving while contending that the accommodation was not an assault on Canadian society as a whole.[84]

Examples of clothing based on cultural or religious requirements involve the wearing of face covering or the wearing of head dresses. This has been the case with the Islamic requirement for women to dress modestly in which some Muslim women choose to wear a hijab head covering or a full-face burqa. Orthodox Sikh

---

[84] https://leaderpost.com/opinion/editorials/gender-segregated-swim-for-refugee-children-nothing-to-get-upset-about

men have also requested to wear their headdress in non-conventional setting such as military or police despite the required uniformity as per official dress codes based on Eurocentric policies. These types of requests to accommodate cultural and religious dress requirements have been a common occurrence within Canada and many other white settler societies in recent decades due to multiculturalism. Accommodating a special need relating to a piece of clothing can seem rather trivial in a society that promotes diversity and inclusiveness, but often these requests for a reasonable accommodation comes with conditions that challenge Eurocentric social norms that reflect whiteness. When a Muslim woman wishes to wear her hijab or burqa while working at a job, such as a teacher, nurse or public servant, then this may challenge a Eurocentric social norm. Likewise, when a Sikh man wishes to wear his turban while serving as a police officer or military member then this also may challenge a social norm within a white settler society. The trivial nature of such simple requests – as these clothing ones – wouldn't necessarily disrupt society or cause any undue hardship to non-adherents as they are merely a small part of a diverse multicultural society that is supposed to be inclusive and accommodating.

Multiculturalism and the diversity it produces has now become the standard for determining whether or not reasonable accommodation is required when white social norms conflict with an individual's right to freedom. If an accommodation is therefore simple enough to fulfill then it must be satisfied despite causing a disruption to a Eurocentric social norm so as to keep with the concept of individual freedoms. The social norms that are likely to interfere with the liberties of someone are the ones that are based off of what has become expected in a European colonized society that endorses and enforces whiteness. So now these white social norms can be considered a barrier to diversity and inclusiveness: diversity and inclusiveness are something that must go hand and hand with multiculturalism. This is where the conflict between accommodating a simple request and measuring it against what is considered to be a Eurocentric social norm. Using the concept of European colonization and a society that is based off whiteness, it can now be said that cultural and religious minorities are victims of these social norms and these social norms are therefore oppressing them due to the whiteness that the social norms represent.

Some requests for reasonable accommodation can extend beyond a simple request regarding the wearing of a certain piece of clothing. Requests, such as allowing space and time for religious worship or prayers at the workplace, may arise despite any social norms that endorse or suggest the need for secularism. This has been witnessed in many white settler societies where Muslims have petitioned the need to have prayer areas and special times for prayers at the workplace or educational institutions. In many cases these requests have been made to an employer as a reasonable accommodation under the terms of a constitutional right to freedom of religion. Employers who hire Muslims have faced this situation and were compelled to accommodate their needs, and sometimes by government intervention. In cases where there was government intervention, by way of human rights commissions or other quasi branches of government, the result was that employers were ordered to provide such accommodations so therefore it is highly recommended that employers comply.[85] When employers decide that they must capitulate and provide the special accommodation, it is often done simply to avoid the aggravation of dealing with any quasi government agency and the potential negative publicity from arguing against it. The mainstream media is generally quick to pickup on a story that appears to have an underdog-employee who is being exploited by a corporation, especially a large corporation. Media outlets often run stories about how groups of people are oppressed and how this oppression amounts to discrimination and racism. Stories like this appeal to people's emotions and create victims while garnering a demand for change. Employers generally don't want or need any bad publicity that paints them as being insensitive to the religious needs of someone or depicts them as being racist.

When reasonable accommodation for religious reasons is sought there then becomes a paradigm where one level involves minimal interference with social norms and one level where undue hardship can occur and greatly disrupt social norms. Minimal interference from reasonable accommodation is seen when a religious piece of clothing is worn such as a burqa, hijab or turban. This action doesn't necessarily place the social norms of white settler societies in a situation of ill repute, but when a request of an employer to provide a prayer room and allow special prayer times is made, the social norm of secularism is now challenged thereby placing it into a perceived position of disrepute. It's generally easy enough for a multicultural society to accept the concept of religious attire being worn in public, but it may be another for the elements of secularism to become shattered all in the name of reasonable accommodation. Freedom of religion is a core element that defines individual liberties in white settler societies, but with freedom of religion comes secularism which enables freedom *from* religion if someone so wishes. Shattering the concept of secularism is what can make the idea of reasonable accommodation controversial while also opening up the doors to accusations of racism.

---

[85] https://hiring.monster.ca/employer-resources/workforce-management/workplace-diversity/religious-accomodation-at-work/

Freedom of religion now becomes a binary issue consisting of the need to have it as a social norm and a need to repudiate it in order to be free from it, therefore creating a social dilemma that requires the tipping of a scale based on constitutional rights. When examining how constitutional rights are to be applied in society, the general test is that the right be considered as an individual one and then applied as such.[86] The irony now surfaces when the power of the collective drowns out the rights of an individual and creates collective based rights, representing a group, as opposed to the rights of the individual. Collective based rights are prime pickings for politicians because the politicians are now guaranteed the votes from those within that collective group if they advocate for them. The power of the media in portraying the narrative of how a collective group of people might be oppressed by a Eurocentric social norm further highlights the allure of the cause. Politicians step up and make a claim that they can solve the problem and ameliorate the issues while the media provides coverage of a story where an oppressed group of people now acquired equal constitutional protection thanks to diversity and inclusiveness due to multiculturalism. The news story is satisfying to the general public and the politician has been revered as a warrior of the oppressed. It now appears that egalitarianism has been advanced and that an oppressed group has received reconciliation. But this is nowhere near what egalitarianism should be based on how individual rights are defined. The main reason that an individual was granted the so-called right to wear a certain piece of religious attire, or given the so-called right to special prayer times and have access to a prayer room in the workplace, is because the *collective* demanded the right based on constitutional grounds. Multiculturalism creates a situation where being a victim is more powerful through the *collective* voices demanding social change, and change will more likely be accepted if the general public feels that groups of people are being victimized and oppressed by Eurocentric social norms. The general public want to hear successful stories of how the underdog has been granted justice because it's a feel good thing that makes people feel as if though society is racially equitable.

Unlike some high profile cases that fought their way through the court system, issues relating to religious attire and prayer related matters are now fought through the media and by special interest groups who lobby the government. Forcing capitulation based on diversity and inclusiveness, especially due to multiculturalism, is perhaps the simplest methods for a collective to achieve their means. Demonstrating that the request for reasonable accommodation will not cause any undo hardship to the non-adherent member of society makes the request

---

[86] https://www.justice.gc.ca/eng/csj-sjc/just/05.html

seem even less demanding and therefore more reasonable. The premise that it shouldn't be an issue if someone wishes to wear a turban, hijab, burqa, if someone wishes to pray openly at a workplace or if women and men be segregated is the principle basis to the argument used by those advocating the request. When someone opposes a request for reasonable accommodation it is rather effortless to paint the opposer as a bigot or racist and claim that their opposition to the request is frivolous and constitutionally unfounded. By claiming that any opposition to a reasonable accommodation is due to some kind of racist motivation fundamentally ends the debate immediately. The opposer of the reasonable accommodation is now in a defensive position baring all the onus to justify their stance while the collective, who's seeking the accommodation, simply claims that they're being further victimized by racism and bigotry in a Eurocentric white settler society. This racial victimization reinforces the collective's request while garnering attention from the media and politicians and this is crucial in silencing the opposition. This occurs even despite an argument that the opposition to the accommodations has absolutely nothing to do with bigotry or racism and that the opposition is only based on grounds of secularism. Opposition specifying freedoms from religion should be deemed as a valid argument, but nevertheless becomes inconsequential when going up against accusations of racism and bigotry. Secularism now dissolves as a social norm, under the weight of apparent collective victimization, and a revolution of the oppressed takes the forefront undermining individual rights.

Oppression by a colonial social norm

Baltej Singh Dhillon is a Canadian who was pivotal in challenging a Eurocentric social norm in Canada when he requested to wear his turban and sport his full beard as part of his Royal Canadian Mounted Police uniform. Dhillon's request was initially denied due to policies related to strict standards regarding the official uniform even though the RCMP initiated an affirmative action program aimed at hiring visible minorities such as Dhillon. The RCMP wanted to implement racial diversity into its police force, but it wasn't prepared for the challenges to the Eurocentric social norms that such an implementation would entail. The concept of implementing racial diversity into the force was a by-product of multiculturalism and it was meant to show how diversity and inclusiveness is an integral element of contemporary Canadian society. By this very notion, the RCMP indirectly invited the dispute and controversy that the Dhillon case accompanied thus creating victim status for Dhillon before he even began his battle against a Eurocentric social norm involving the RCMP. The RCMP never knew it at the time, but they were inviting someone to claim victim status after the force's initiative to hire visible minorities as a plan to implement diversity. They clearly never thought through what the process of affirmative action would entail, thereby suggesting that it was entirely lip-service by the upper echelon of the RCMP and that the entire notion of affirmative action was politically encouraged and staged.

Had the RCMP gave genuine thought to their diversity plan, they should have been able to foresee the potential issue and made allowances for it. This would have nevertheless been a form of advance capitulation, but it would have prevented the subsequent various legal claims and accusations of racism that occurred because of the initial refusal to allow Dhillon to wear his beard and turban as part of the uniform. The Dhillon case nevertheless set a precedent that has now extended to allowing Muslim women to wear hijabs as part of the official police uniform and has encouraged the police force to specifically recruit them as a show of diversity. [87] As cultural diversity progresses across Canada and other white settler countries, there will certainly be fully vailed women serving as police officers donning the full burqa as part of their uniform as a means to attack Eurocentric social norms and to demonstrate the diversity and inclusiveness that must go hand-and-hand with multiculturalism. Religious attire that was once outside of the cultural landscape of a white settler society is now becoming a new social norm as many police forces seek out such persons to display how they are capitulating with cultural diversity due to large scale immigration that results from multiculturalism. This benefits the police force by allowing them to cash in on the virtue bandwagon and let's them avoid being labelled as culturally insensitive or racist. The concept of how social norms are changing is also extended to many other organizations besides police forces. The Canadian Armed Forces and all civilian services in Canada have also adopted similar recruiting methods and special allowances for religious attire to be worn with any prescribed uniform or dress codes. [88] [89]

Many private organizations also allow the wearing of religious attire that once contravened the social norms of a white settler country. Allowing the wearing of religious attire by private organizations is largely a choice on their own accord, but it can however be heavily influenced by the fear of what the repercussions might be if they refused to accommodate it. Reverberations can occur that result in someone, or an organization, being labeled as culturally insensitive and or racist, is often enough of a deterrent from refusing a reasonable accommodation request. It's therefore generally easy for a request for reasonable accommodation to be attained without any form of governmental intervention. Private organizations are often

---

[87] https://www.cbc.ca/news/politics/rcmp-diversity-policy-hijab-1.3733829
[88] https://www.canada.ca/en/services/defence/caf/military-identity-system/dress-manual/chapter-2/section-3.html
[89] https://ipolitics.ca/2015/03/11/niqab-welcome-in-federal-public-service-clement-thompson/

willing to capitulate to such requests in an attempt avoid a negative media portrayal or a bad public image. The same scenario can occur when private organizations face requests to accommodate religious prayers within their workplace. There are many instances where businesses in secular white settler societies have been required to provide special prayer times and prayer spaces for their employees in order to meet the terms of reasonable accommodations. In some cases, businesses were order by human rights tribunals to provide such reasonable accommodations, and in other cases, the businesses simply complied with employees' requests.[90] When businesses actually defy the elements of what a Eurocentric social norm is considered to be under the concept of secularism in a white settler society and accommodate a special need, this can certainly appear to be heroic and in compliance with what multiculturalism is said to represent.

· · · · · · · · · · · · · ·

Regardless of whether or not a business wishes to accommodate the special needs of a person's religion, secularism should dictate that the separation of religion and state be paramount in order to ensure that democracy is instituted on such a level that individual rights are respected. Individual rights relating to secularism should (in theory) ensure that freedom of religion safeguards people from any influence that religion may have on politics. When legislators get involved in dictating that reasonable accommodations must involve the right to pray in the work place then this amounts to religious interference with individual rights.[91] The rights of a collective group have now trumped any individual rights that a secular democracy should offer thereby eroding the freedom *from* religion. Further to this is the matter that collective rights are only being enforced under the guise of freedom of religion which creates the dilemma suggesting that any opposition to this collectivism is deemed as undemocratic. Multiculturalism has allowed the rights of the collective to be at the forefront of political policies, just the same as they did during early white European settlement that oppressed the Indigenous people when European religions were considered a paramount aspect of a functioning society.

Any opposition to collectivism that is deemed to be undemocratic takes on a new form by insinuating that the opposition is rooted in racism due to the colonial structure of contemporary white settler society. This concept of contemporary colonialism, disguised as *diversity,* makes it easy to use a race base argument to

---

[90] https://www.nccm.ca/wp-content/uploads/2014/03/NCCM-Employer-GUIDE-PF.pdf
[91] https://www.thestar.com/news/queenspark/2017/03/23/muslim-prayers-in-schools-get-provincial-endorsement-following-intense-meeting.html

perpetuate victimization demonstrating that the current white settler society implicitly summons up racism as a default position. Racism by default is the underlining factor when critical race theorists use colonialism as a basis for justifying their contention that white settler societies are inherently racist. So any opposition to a request for reasonable accommodation is considered to be a result of this inherent racism and results in victimization for the group being denied their request. This inherent racism is also manifested through covert actions due to racism that is ingrained within the fabric of white settler societies. The covert actions that are demonstrated with the opposition to a request for reasonable accommodations are deemed to be rooted in racism because of the colonial structured system that places whiteness as the baseline for what the social norms are in a so-called democratic society. Using this concept as a method of creating a victim is rather simplistic when racial inequality is used as a foundation for an argument of oppression and how whiteness is the perpetrator of such oppression. The opposition to any request for religious accommodation is therefore essentially grounded within the fundamental racism that is ingrained in white settler societies through *whiteness*. This *whiteness* is manifested either overtly or covertly and can be perceived as racist either way. The overt racism is rather easy to detect whereas it entails direct and open disdain for something based only on factors of race alone.

Overt racism is without a doubt the most unacceptable excuse for rejecting a reasonable accommodation for religious purposes, but it's very unlikely that even the most racist person in contemporary multicultural societies would ever use such an open racist reason for any type of refusal and thereby knowingly create a victim. In contemporary white settler societies practicing multiculturalism, overt racism is strongly condemned and contravenes any notion of egalitarianism and is actively discouraged by many social standards of inclusiveness. Government, media, law enforcement and the education system vigorously combats any form of overt racism by strongly discouraging it and by using equality legislation to enforce laws against discrimination and against hate crimes. So it should then be relatively easy to identify and combat racism in a contemporary multicultural white settler society and to ensure that egalitarianism is paramount thus ensuring that nobody is a victim of overt racism. This in theory should set a standard that a request for reasonable accommodation, based on religion, will be considered without issue. If there are human rights commissions enforcing equality legislation, police enforcing hate crime laws and the media acting as the voice of the citizenry, then this should be a strong deterrent for people to be dissuaded from engaging in overt racism. A contemporary multicultural white settler society doesn't always focus on elements of overt actions of racism due to the far more concerning elements of covert racism. It's essentially the aspect of this covert racism that is a driving force in creating victims of discrimination and it doesn't necessarily take an open or outright instance of actual racism to create a victim anymore. By simply suggesting that racially marginalized groups of people are being oppressed because of systemic or institutional forms of discrimination – that are believed to be inherent in a white settler society despite multiculturalism – covert racism is now a concern.

Using the aspect of covert racism allows for insinuated allegations that racism exists even when there are no actual physical signs of it. This is what can happen when a multicultural white settler society is tolerant and is progressing forward in terms of inclusiveness and egalitarianism. If a group feels left out of the social progress and feels as if they aren't benefiting by having their special interest recognized as a reasonable accommodation, then it would logically stand to reason that perhaps they are being covertly discriminated against by the inherent forces of colonial whiteness and the Eurocentric social norms it demands. But when there are no signs of actual physical discrimination or open acts of racism, a collective group can still insist that due to the initial social foundations of white settler societies – being founded on principles of Eurocentric whiteness – discrimination and racism can inherently exist by default: this default is the covert racism that can replace the overt racism when such overt racism is not physically present due to systemic or institutional factors that mask covert racism. It now becomes possible to claim genuine status as a victim of racial inequality, and if this victim status is disputed for any reason, then the disputer is simply part of the problem due to inherent covert racism. Covert racism can now be a powerful weapon in the fight against Eurocentric white based social norms while allowing for collective dissent against any logical opposition to requests of an accommodation that might cause undue hardship to individuals.

Unconscious racial bias

Unconscious bias is a conspicuous term that is often thrown around by social justice advocates who espouse that there is an inherent racial bias within a white settler society. This inherent racial bias stems from a precipitable controlling element of a dominant faction in which the society is constructed upon and it's often used by politicians to cash in on political virtue. A dominant faction can encompass many facets whereas race, gender, economic status and many other social components can construct an acceptable conception of social normality. When this conception of a social component is not conducive –
therefore questioning a social normality – this can create a situation that defies the acceptable conception or definition of the word *social normality*. Through defying the acceptable conception, or definition of a social normality, the perception of

such a social normality may influence how someone views and or concludes events related to that social normality. This is where the element of overtness and covertness comes into play. The conception of an unconscious bias can therefore be a crucial component in defining covert discrimination despite a lack of authentic correlation between the two terms.

The political nature of the two terms creates a fertile environment therefore constructing a prime opportunity for politicians and social justice advocates to use the terms interchangeably and in unison. The term covert racism now becomes a neologism that is thrown about whenever there is a need to enact a social cause related to a matter of alleged discrimination or social injustice by insinuating that covertness is actually overtness or vice versa. The standard of proof relating to an alleged discrimination is now lowered and doesn't require any corresponding corroboration to demonstrate that there has been a discriminatory act. Regardless if there is no actual overt racism, covert racism can be used as an explanation thereby skewing the two terms due to the premise that white settler societies are inherently racist. Using this neologism allows for an easier classification of a *victim* and further deters any opposition to a claim of victim status. In claiming that one is victimized by a covert/unconscious act, there is no refutation available for the person or entity being accused of perpetuating an alleged covert/unconscious act toward someone else. It can now be argued that the discriminatory act is an inherent result of a white settler society that is constructed upon social normalities that are unconsciously designed to oppress the non-adherents. Non-adherents are those who were not privy to creating the very social constructs that form a white settler society and who benefit from the social constructs as such. In other words, non-white people are automatically discriminated against due the the social structure of a white settler society that perpetuates an unconscious bias resulting in covert racism, even when nothing overt occurs.

The racial context of unconscious biases

A simple internet search for the definition of racism defines it as a prejudice, discrimination, or antagonism directed against someone of a different race based on the belief that one's own race is superior. This common definition essentially suggests that it should apply to a broad spectrum of people from all races, creeds and cultures by holding that there's no specific race that is the sole perpetrator of racism. There is however a contemporary version of racism that has captured the intellectual delight of critical race theorists in white settler societies where the contemporary definition has its developing roots. This modern definition stems from the ideology that criticizing the weaknesses of non-white cultures is an inherent act of covert racism based on an ethnocentric European model of whiteness and the professed privileges that accompany such whiteness. To exemplify this modern definition of racism and how the criticisms of other cultures, due to ethnocentric whiteness, we only need to examine nineteenth century General Sir Charles James Napier and his quote regarding the Indian practice of widow burning:

Be it so. This burning of widows is your custom; prepare the funeral pile. But my nation has also a custom. When men burn women alive we hang them, and confiscate all their property. My carpenters shall therefore erect gibbets on which to hang all concerned when the widow is consumed. Let us all act according to national customs….

The mere act of criticizing a non-white culture as being inferior, barbaric or culturally obsolete is contemporarily misconstrued as being racist due to an ethnocentric viewpoint that is propagated by inherent whiteness. Critical race theorists hold that this inherent whiteness is a direct result of Eurocentrism which embraces a colonial/imperialistic nuance thus disseminating covert racism unwittingly throughout the human psyche. Someone who construes simple factual statements criticizing alien cultures as potentially barbaric and not conducive with a white settler society that is socially and politically progressive can be accused of manifesting racism that stems from an unconscious bias. The unconscious bias will then be a breeding ground for covert racism that is manifested in subtle ways by promoting whiteness.

Chapter 9: The victims of a white settler society due to exclusive whiteness.

> *Using colonization as a core feature of an argument is rather simple and doesn't require any special education, training or mandatory apprenticeship.*

The key to success for a modern-day revolution is not warfare, weapons or civil disobedience, but rather a proclamation of victimization and the best way to make the claim of victim in a white settler society is through *colonialism*. European colonization is the foundation for every claim of contemporary victimization involving the oppression of a marginalized group whether it be racial, gender, sexual or economic. When someone wishes to express their discontent with egalitarianism in a white settler society, virtually every claim of discrimination or injustice can be attributed to European colonization – if someone is so inclined to pursue that school of thought. The people who are very inclined to pursue that school of thought are those who push the racial oppression and injustice angle to show that colonialism creates victims. Critical race theorists use European colonization as the core principles of many of their arguments as to why injustices and discrimination occur within white settler societies. Using colonization as a core feature of an argument is rather simple and doesn't require any special education, training or mandatory apprenticeship. It could be as simple as reading a few books from the local library, listening to radio talk shows, watching the main stream media or finding mentorship. The latter is perhaps the most common instance as it mostly occurs at post-secondary institutions within the humanities and social sciences. Essentially every post-secondary course within the humanities and social sciences consist of some form of critical race theory that espouses the concept of oppressor versus the oppressed and does so through a concept of inherent racial injustices that are ingrained within a white settler society. But it doesn't however take any level of education to adopt this method of societal critique, it merely takes a simple aptitude to embrace a stance of social justice and to perceive the entire white settler society through the lens of race therefore creating a victim base.

The language of Victims

Claiming the status of victim is not a very complicated task if someone has a collective group of potential victims at their side. It can be more difficult for the individual to espouse victim status when they are in the game alone and up against barriers that seem to enclose them in, especially when the barriers are considered systemic or institutional. Some basic tenants of victimology suggest that there are a few steps for the individual to take in order to be classified as a victim within a white settler society. First, there has to be an injustice committed against the person that was beyond their control,[92] which could include a crime, systemic offence relating to discrimination or a civil infraction such as a motor vehicle accident or property violation. These three are just the tip of the iceberg as to what an actual injustice could be against someone seeking victim status. Multiculturalism can pave the way for contemporary victims to have a whole host of social tools to use when claiming victim status and many of these tools are state sponsored. After someone is victimized, they must have some form of recognition as a victim, which could come from family, friends or official state acknowledgement. Recognition from family or friends is generally simple, but official state acknowledgement could be somewhat laborious, especially if the state is a white settler society. Victim services are often government funded, but also

---

[92] https://www.justice.gc.ca/eng/rp-pr/cj-jp/victim/res-rech/p6.html

rely on private donations thereby encountering financial strains from time-to-time. Scarcity in funding or donations could impede the ability of victim services to serve victims accordingly, therefore giving the impression that the state doesn't care about their interests.

Another reason why victims may seem left out by the state is because the state apparatus is often weighed down in bureaucracy and victim support systems may unknowingly overlook a victim due to such a weight down. Staffing resources and a shortage of skilled service workers may also be prevalent within victim services, especially when such services are government funded and cutbacks are a results of fiscal restructuring. When a victim finds that they are being neglected within the state apparatus and or find that they are lacking recognition from friends or family, the media can often play an important role in offering the victim some much needed acknowledgement. The media's role in offering a victim recognition can be a pivotal moment where the victim attains the necessary acknowledgement as a victim while exposing the state system that may have ignored them. The media has the capability to reach people en masse and can act as an advocate for the victim and use the victim's story to create a venue for social solicitude. This is accomplished through the use of specific language containing words with the suffix of "phobia", which can be very influential politically, emotionally and socially.

The phobia concept(s)

The phobia concept has had a profound influence on language relating to victimization and how it can be used as *capital* by individuals who hold the perception that a society oppresses specific groups of people. Using the phobia concept as a form of *capital* is done by individuals who wish to convey their discontent of social situations that they believe are oppressive. By classifying a person as part of the collective – due to oppression of course – a phobia term is an excellent means to do so as it automatically places a lone person into a collective victim group. It would ostensibly suggest that the phobia is a result of inherent and intentional oppression on the part of a dominant group and that such oppression is a result of an irrational fear of the alleged oppressed person or group. The alleged oppressed person or group can now classify themselves according to their selected phobia and then claim their place within a collective category of victimhood. The distinction between exactly when the phobia designation becomes a collective matter occurs when an individual's social disruption is deemed to be a result of their innate belonging to a collective group in one way or another. The innate belonging could include, race, religion, language, culture, gender, sexual orientation or a whole host of other attributes, be it physical or otherwise. The social disruption could include an array of actions that are deemed unjust and or discriminatory thus being classified as a phobia on the part of the accused oppressor ensuring that the victim's phobia is inline with a collective phobia that is used to highlight an alleged social injustice. Nevertheless, once a person does however receive the recognition of victim status from state and non-state players, they are now supported by a collective group and can begin to move forward with the process of building their victimized position within society and the state system. The position that is being built is based on compensation, which is the ultimate end goal for victims in order to regain what has been lost due to the victimization. This is where multiculturalism allows for popular phobias like xenophobia, Islamaphobia and theophobia, but claiming a phobia status in this manner is only possible when a person claims to belong to an oppressed group of people who are victimized by society; in this case, a white settler society. These kinds of phobias were certainly present during early white settler immigration where colonial whites feared those who were different from them and where governmental policies reflected those fears accordingly. Victimization resulting from a person's race is an irony that can ostensibly occur in a multicultural society due to the possibility of racial polarization. This victimization through polarization then opens the door to a concept of racial fluidity to counter any racial polarization created by the colonial establishment thereby allowing victims of racism to find refuge in a chosen racial identity.

• • • • • • • • • • • • • •

Whiteness and the one drop rule

The one drop rule is a fascinating element of social justice whereas it dictates that the person with merely *one* sole drop of non-white lineage can automatically claim the innate right to identify as an exclusive member of that lineage in which they have the one drop of. The one drop rule has its best known origins in the American political and cultural systems when it was used to identify those of black ancestry by inferring that people who possessed one drop of black African blood was therefore legally considered to be African American. The one drop rule is a prime example of a white man's regulation aimed at specifying when and where a non-white person fits into the social structure of society therefore preserving the white built structure. The very nature of the one drop rule reeks of racism, but is nevertheless used as a component of celebration amongst modern social justice warriors and those who advocate racial equality through racial distinction. The one drop rule clearly lays out who is white by detailing who is not white. The one drop rule places individuals into a racial non-white category thus ensuring the legal and social separation between whites and non-whites. In the case of the United States, persons with at least one ancestor of sub-Saharan African lineage can be considered black: even if they are majority white.[93] President Barack Obama has a black father and a white mother, but is exclusively noted for being the first African American elected to the Oval Office. The mainstream media never celebrated that a half black/white man was elected as president nor did the mainstream media ever suggest that President Obama was never really a black man in terms of full one hundred percent blackness. If the mainstream media was to even fathom the thought of doing this it would surely create an outrage resulting in accusations of racism and intolerance. President Obama's blackness was a major asset for the mainstream media as it was key in promoting how racial equality was prevalent in America and how political progress has finally claimed a stake in the inexhaustible battle for racial justice.

Conceptualizing President Obama with how Canada views Indigenous people is where the one drop rule can be examined and placed into a social context. The Métis people of Canada are folks who have a bloodline that identifies them as being part Indigenous and part non-Indigenous. An offensive and relic term with racist connotations that was often used to identify such Indigenous folks was *halfbreed*. This term is no longer politically correct and has been replaced with Métis, but examining the term can help in reaching an understanding of why it was used. The offensive nature of the term is what distinguished the Indigenous person from the white person because it painted the Indigenous person as inferior to whites. The term allowed the white man to attach a social stigma on Indigenous people as persons who were socially, politically and in every way fundamentally subservient to the white colonizers who held the balance of societal power. The one drop rule allowed the white man to attach a social stigma to any person who wasn't white and who wasn't privileged enough to belong to the power structure of the colonial rulers. This ensured that the white colonizers could maintain their social power and ensure that race would always be forefront in deciding where a person stood on the ladder of the colonial political structure. It also ensured that whiteness was preserved and held to the highest social standards thus protecting the racial hierarchy demanded by a colonial white settler society.

---

[93] https://en.m.wikipedia.org/wiki/One-drop_rule

Even today this hierarchy of whiteness is still maintained within the British royal family despite allowing the marriage of non-royals and non-whites to take place among them. How this privilege among the royals has gone unnoticed among social justice warriors, who demand mass immigration and open borders, is certainly a question that has never been put to the test. Recognizing whiteness within a European colonized society is as simple as looking at the surface elements of it and how it functions. There are many examples of how white privilege is prevalent in a white settler society, such as Canada, which includes the many ways whiteness has purposely created a social disadvantage for the Indigenous people. By clearly specifying who's ostensibly racially pure and who has non-whiteness – through a system that evidently places whites within a racially pure category – there should be an obvious channel of official protest for those who oppose the state conception of white colonialism; one would think. Policies such as this specifying someone's race can be used as a means of state sponsored discrimination via laws that support segregation and other social programs aimed at dividing whites and non-whites. The inevitable question of who the Indigenous people are can be subjective or objective depending upon the point of analysis you undertake and what elements of it are biased by whiteness.

Defining Indigenous

The term Indigenous is something that needs some analysis that will ensure a clear and concise definition. Simply assuming that Indigenous people implies someone who is Indigenous to the land may be somewhat of a misnomer if you were to compare the particular lands that Indigenous inhabitants have or are currently occupying. For example, it's clearly without a doubt that First Nations, Inuit and Métis people are all collectively considered Indigenous to the lands of Canada by virtue of the fact that they all had a connection to the lands prior to European colonization. Using the backdrop of European colonization as a standard in defining the term Indigenous person, is the key in deciding whether it is an objective approach rather than a subjective one because there's no doubt that Canada's first Nations, Métis and Inuit people had pre-European colonization connections to the lands. Yes of course the Métis people didn't come into existence until European colonization, but they still have more of a connection to the land than the white colonizers had. So using the objective standard of land connection, the Indigenous people in Canada are clearly defined without any doubt as Indigenous persons. On top of this, they have official recognition under the constitution as well as many pieces of legislation, treaties and other governmental regulations identifying them as such. Colonization is largely known to have been perpetrated by white European powers in an attempt to reap the resources of the desired lands. In order to do this, the colonizers would occupy the lands and establish their presence through instituting official outposts, trading posts and other governmental methods that demonstrated a social dominant presence and superiority. The distinction between the colonizers and the Indigenous inhabitants were clear-cut so there shouldn't be any issue in defining who an Indigenous person is: and in this case, an Indigenous person is someone who suffered at the the hands of European colonizers by losing their inherent connection to their lands through colonialism. But what if the term Indigenous can be somewhat fluid? Fluid in the sense that it was interchangeable or the choice of the person to be identified as a member of a race and then be viewed as perfectly acceptable by society.

Transracial identification

The term *transracial* is certainly a radical concept when addressing the issue of defining a person's race because it allows the person to make a completely subjective choice as of who they are racially. Although this isn't necessarily a common theme expressed in contemporary Canadian society, it has been a noticeable element within other aspects of society and has its own recognition from politicians and advocates alike. Self-identifying as the gender of choice is the new craze that has swept over Canada forcing politicians into a dilemma where they essentially compete with one another for who will be the most socially inclusive and who will gain the most votes from their appearance of compassion and political correctness. The dilemma for politicians arises when there is opposition to the *self-identifying* demand, which is usually quickly followed by accusations of some kind of phobia, bigotry or social insensitivity. The outcome of politicians appearing insensitive to the *self-identifying* needs of people is the same as accusations of racism, similarly as if they were to ignore any cultural, religious or racial needs of non-whites. Although this concept of self-identifying as a specific race may seem somewhat absurd it's actually something that has occurred in the past; albeit not frequently but enough to garner recognition from social justice advocates. Take for example the famous 1950s singer Johnny Otis who was a son of white Greek immigrants, but lived his life more or less as a black person. Otis was considered by most to be a light skinned black man who married his high school sweetheart (who was black) and would stay in segregated black hotels with his black band mates when on tour and who lived in segregated black housing with his family.[94] The idea that Johnny Otis could live as a black man is not a social travesty whatsoever, and by all means he should have the choice to do so if he so desires. Supporters of racial identification through choice will argue that race is fluid essentially making race nothing more than a social construct. The fluidity of race can therefore result from societal expectations whereas someone is benefiting from their race whether it's biological or chosen. When Johnny Otis was perceived as a black man he then met the societal expectations of how a black musical performer was to perform thereby completing the social construct that racial fluidity perpetuates.

This allowed Otis to easily transform from being a white man into a black man with complete social approval and with complete access to the culture of African Americans while nobody gave it a second thought. Johnny Otis's race, between being white and identifying as black, were fluid meaning that there were no barriers or social constraints that assigned him to a race or culture solely based upon the colour of his skin. The *fluid* aspect of the term *racially fluid* implies that race is like water and it can easily move from place to place because it's not solid, certain or permanently assigned. Johnny Otis can simply move between race just as water can simply move between close knit rocks and other tight spaces. Racial fluidity basically allows someone to choose their race as they see fit provided they use the conception of *self-identifying* as the means to do so.

Another notable example of someone who is white, but chose to identify as black thus giving credence to the term *transracial person,* is Rachel Dolezal. Rachel Dolezal is perhaps the most infamous person who coined the term *transracial* into a contemporary locution that is inline with the postulation of racial fluidity that justified Johnny Otis's choice of public representation. Dolezal, much the same as Otis, was married to a black person, worked with black folks and related to being black and took on the physical characteristics of a black person. Unlike Otis however, Dolezal was outed by a reporter who confronted her with accusation of lying and for misappropriating a race she didn't belong to. Despite this, Dolezal still maintains that race is fluid and that she has felt like a black person since she was a child and has compared herself to Caitlyn Jenner claiming that race is not in your DNA but is rather like gender or religion[95] therefore fluid. In many ways Rachel Dolzel made the most out of her transformation just like Johnny Otis did in that she attended a traditionally black college, had black siblings who were adopted, married a black man and worked in an industry (NAACP) that was

---

[94] https://www.cnn.com/2018/03/02/us/racial-fluidity/index.html
[95] https://www.nzherald.co.nz/world/news/article.cfm?c_id=2&objectid=11839560

primarily black. This gave her the persona of being a legitimate black person and gave her full justification to claim social status as a person of African ancestry despite having white birth parents. Dolezal has no regrets about her decision in life regarding the appropriation of the African American culture and was quick to point this out to Dr. Phil as simply being *transracial*.[96] It could be said that nowadays Rachel Dolezal is an advocate for racial fluidity[97] and for all contemporary purposes there's perhaps no reason why she shouldn't be able to identify as the race she so desires and there shouldn't be any reason for an inclusive society, such as America, to turn their backs on someone like Dolezal. Dolezal has more or less become an icon for the contemporary social justice warriors who want to use race as a means to demonstrate how oppression is prevalent in today's society. This has allowed the contemporary social justice warriors to ignore the fact Dolezal is biologically white therefore making the issue a moot point and not worthy of further acknowledgement. Any attempt to draw attention to the fact the Dolezal is knowingly appropriating a culture for her own selfish means will surely result in accusations of racism, insensitivity and bigotry. The example of how Johnny Otis and Rachel Dolezal harnessed the ability to tap into a fragment of society that would over look the theft of a culture – a culture that has suffered discrimination – shows that society can be blinded by their own push to achieve racial equality through racial inclusiveness and tolerance.

The notion of racial fluidity is a concept that is perhaps more applicable to people of mixed race heritages. Take for example President Barack Obama – who has a black father and a white mother and who identifies as black – is known to be a black man by the vast majority of people if you were to ask them. President Obama is certainly always referred to as the first black president and is never referred to as the first racially mixed one. But if Obama was to decide that he wanted to tap into the white aspect of his heritage he should therefore be fully entitled to do so pursuant to the notion of racial fluidity. Obama however has essentially lived his life as a black man, and has clearly identified as such, therefore appealing to the greater notion of him being fully black and never having any inclination of reminding people that he is just as biologically white as he is black. Using the concept of racial fluidity it can be surmised that Barack Obama has many social components in common with Johnny Otis and Rachel Dolezal that assist in identifying as black. Components such as where they chose to live, go to school,

---

[96] https://www.drphil.com/shows/transracial-in-america-the-rachel-dolezal-controversy/

[97] https://www.independent.co.uk/news/people/rachel-dolezal-white-woman-black-racial-fluidity-accepted-transracial-naacp-a7653131.html

where they worked and racial identification were all social aspects that gave these three folks the ability to create the persona as being black. Unlike Johnny Otiss and Rachel Dolezal, Barack Obama does however have a genuine biological heritage that entitles him to identify as black according to the one drop rule. This is where racial fluidity begins to differentiate itself from the *transracial* notion put forward by Rachel Dolezal.

Theft by cultural identity

Arguing that racial fluidity alone entitles someone to easily and simply identify as the race they so desire is actually disingenuous to those who are from mixed racial heritage. Kramer, Burke and Charles (2015) suggest that racial fluidity is best reserved for those people of mixed race because it allows them to straddle and/or cross social barriers that may arise due to a crisis of identity.[98] From the perspective of a social justice warrior who advocates that race is a social construct aimed at classifying people for the purposes of oppression, allowing mixed race folks to choose their race might be a great solution if one racial aspect had a social advantage over another. Having the option to select your race might have its advantages socially whereas you can apply the concept of fluidity and change things up according to how you want to be perceived. If choosing one race allows you to gain a social advantage, such as obtaining specific housing aimed at assisting minorities, or obtaining employment via affirmative action or gaining admission into university, then perhaps racial fluidity can be a racial equalizer. But in all reality this example of racial fluidity should only be applicable to those of genuine mixed races that have experienced racial polarization due to systemic and institutional circumstances. So when a person essentially identifies as being a member of a certain race in which they have no biological claim to, this now becomes cultural appropriation and theft of resources; resources that would have been available to the genuine person of that race, and should be considered pure racism in our contemporary society. The issue of cultural appropriation will inevitably transform into allegations of racism that will ensure even further racial polarization thus defeating the purpose of achieving racial equality.

Johnny Otis and Rachel Dolezel have no biological claim to the race they chose to identify with, but both have obtained social benefits as a result of their chosen racial identity. According to the theory of colonialism, it's the white European people who staked a claim to the Indigenous lands and occupied them. It is also the

---

white Europeans who were benefactors of slavery that oppressed Africans, Indigenous and other people of colour due to laws that prevented racial equality. Therefore it would be completely prudent to conclude that staking a claim to a race that someone has no biological connection to whatsoever is clearly a blatant act of racial/cultural theft. It's perhaps one thing if someone is simply an actor, but even when that someone is white, portraying the role of a non-white is very often deemed an act of racial/cultural theft and further deemed as being racist. It can be clearly stated that proclaiming to be a member of a racial group that someone doesn't belong to is socially improper and should be condemned accordingly.

By justifying or taking the position that it's okay to be transracial, when there's no inherent basis to it, fundamentally creates a situation where you inadvertently approve of cultural appropriation therefore encouraging imposters to abuse any social privileges the oppressed race has achieved or are entitled to, such as affirmative action for example. Take for example in Canada where Indigenous people have special constitutional status, protective legislation that identifies them and many legal court decisions that have been incorporated into common law, all which assist in determining who is Indigenous and what they are entitled to as such. Condemning racial imposters can protect against normalizing negative behaviour that can hurt genuine members of that race, while at the same time, reinforcing who the genuine members of the race are. It should be noted that the case of Johnny Otis was used here only to exemplify how the perception of race can be inflicted by the fluidity of it. Johnny Otis was a successful and very popular musical performer who never made any false claims to bolster his success or image like Rachel Dolezel did. The free market allowed Otis's success due to his musical talent where people paid money to enjoy his music because he was an excellent musician and his benefiting from a perceived racial aspect was not fraudulent like Dolezel. Otis chose to live his life the way he did because he was perhaps comfortable doing so and it was the cohesion between his music and the community who supported him that created his persona. Otis does however demonstrate how racial fluidity can occur in theory from a social justice standpoint.

White Indigenous People! Is this even possible?

We already know who the Indigenous people are in white settler societies such as Canada and what qualifies them to be such persons. Indigenous people are the original inhabitants of a land or territory and their descendants who remain on such lands or territories thereafter. It's generally a straight forward idea that the first occupants of an area are the ones who should be able to stake claim based on Aboriginal status and have their Aboriginal status protected by law thus ensuring their legacy will be continued and respected accordingly with regards to history.[99] Canada has ensured that this idea is followed through official constitutional protection and recognizing the many treaties between colonial powers and the Indigenous people. Using this idea of recognizing original inhabitants of a land or territory, can it be at all possible for there to be *white* Indigenous people? There is an antidote that may hold the supposition that a white person can be considered Aboriginal to a land so long as they hold a connection to that land in the same ways that the traditional Indigenous people of Canada do: A case in point might be the white people of Europe. Referring to the white people of England, who have occupied the country for centuries, as Indigenous people would without a doubt seem ludicrous, but not an unimaginable supposition nonetheless.

This concept can be a very controversial one whereas it suggests that people of white ethnicity are claiming some type of nationhood to a land in which they never had any right to in the first place.[100] Keeping in mind how colonialism is a concept that has been perpetrated by the white man as a tool of oppression, a contemporary ideology of white ethnicity being linked to some sort of Indigenous status makes it a notion that can be considered racist. Take for example British politician Nick Griffin who espoused the idea that the English, Scottish, Welsh and the Irish are the Aboriginal people of Britain. Griffin was swiftly reminded by many folks that this idea was totally nationalistic and reeks of white supremacy. Although the concept of being white indigenous can hold that the island of Britain was first occupied by whites of four different cultures and that this can somehow be compared to the different Indigenous people in North America, contemporary societies of North America and Europe are certainly not ready politically or socially to fathom such a concept and probably never will be due to multiculturalism. There would however be no objection whatsoever if the concept of Indigenous people were applied to Japan, where the first people there to occupy and develop the lands were the Indigenous Japanese and who still reside there today as the mono-ethnic group of people. South and North Korea are also other countries where it could be espoused that those people are also Indigenous. The same goes for China, Saudi Arabia, Iran and other similar countries that have never

[99] https://www.un.org/development/desa/dspd/wp-content/uploads/sites/22/2018/07/Chapter-VIIIndigenous-peoples-and-ethnic-minorities.pdf
[100] https://www.theguardian.com/commentisfree/2010/dec/20/indigenous-britons-far-right

been colonized by white Europeans or whom have never been so politically influenced by whiteness that the Indigenous people were displaced to the point of losing their nationhood as it happened in Canada.

It is without a doubt that the people of the aforementioned countries are the Aboriginal people and have not undergone the colonial transformation to the point that Canada and other white settler countries have when it comes to their Indigenous people. Indigenous is Indigenous and the argument that the ethnic Iranian and Korean people are Aboriginal is certainly fortified in basic common sense. So then why aren't the white people of Great Britain considered indigenous? Well it would be the issue of colonialism and the power it exerted over the Indigenous people of white settler countries who suffered the forced social, political and cultural transformations that decimated their nationhood. The forced social, political and cultural transformations were achieved through the implementation of the *white man's politics* that were the central component of how colonialism was able to defraud the Indigenous people of their self-determination and traditional ways by implementing mass immigration of non-Indigenous people into their land.

Operating under the premise that white settler countries like America and Canada were and are lands built by immigration, would it be safe to suggest that perhaps contemporary immigrants should be required to adhere to the founding principles based off of colonialism? A question like Japan is Japanese and China is Chinese so why can't America/Canada be European is a very perplexing concept that is guaranteed to raise a heated debate. Even conservatives, who may be considered right winged or alt-right, can hold the supposition that a country was and can be founded off of immigration and that immigration can be an underlining principle of that country's heritage. Identifying a unifying foundational *thing* that could make a white colonized country like Canada have a distinguishing identity-trait could be its colonial immigration policies that are hailed as the foundation to building the country and is why multiculturalism is celebrated today. Conservative Matt Walsh is not sure what that *thing* could be in modern American society, but Walsh largely believes that identifying one single trait that would allow or suggest that America is mono-ethnic could be a problem because that's not America's social foundation. Walsh believes that race, skin colour or ethnicity was never the unifying principle and that being so was and is what separates America from every other country and that this created a doctrine of human rights. Today unfortunately, Walsh believes that America lost it's unifying principle[101]: this is where the suggestion could be

---

[101] https://youtu.be/xQQEWGUTCwl

made that Canada was a country founded on the immigration of European settlers so perhaps that should be its identifying and unifying trait and principle. It would appear that this supposition is perhaps accurate due to the fact that multiculturalism encourages mass immigration the same as past colonial immigration did. Canada was indeed a country built off the concept of immigration and contemporary immigration policies all follow that same social pavé: this social pavé is now called multiculturalism instead. Immigration is constantly purported to be a necessity in order to sustain modern society and to ensure that we keep with our heritage of being a nation built by immigrants. So essentially it appears that contemporary immigration, under the concept of multiculturalism, is still a form of mass immigration of non-Indigenous people to further occupy the land and resources and that the unifying *thing* is the government mandated endorsement and celebration of it. This clearly, and unfortunately, makes Canada a nation that still celebrates the white European roots of conquering, occupying and pillaging lands that were stolen from the Indigenous people in order to advance a society that is reflective of European colonialism; but it does so masquerading as multiculturalism and multiculturalism will not benefit the Indigenous people anymore than colonialism did. When Canada declares that a unifying *thing* is the identity as a multicultural country, it is basically the same as celebrating the initial European colonialism – that harmed the Indigenous people – as something positive. So indeed contemporary immigrants are celebrating a colonial concept that harmed the Indigenous people and the governments of today are staunchly championing it by calling it multiculturalism.

Chapter 10: The early immigrants were the workers who built the country: so they say Immigrants are needed because of a labour shortage and because we need continued social and economic growth. Right?

Moreover, tell the next Indigenous person you see that Canada needs loads of more immigrants to fill the labour gap that corporations rave on about – corporations who are a direct product of white European colonialism – and see if the argument gets you any sympathy.

How many times have you heard that immigrants are needed to fill the labour shortage gap and to do the jobs that Canadians don't want to do? Well this is a cliché that is commonly spewed by open border advocates and social justice warriors who are just as quick to claim that foreign workers and workers of colour are being exploited by employers.[102] This exploitation concept isn't new and it's actually an argument made by the infamous 99 percenters who oppose big corporations and the free market. Ironically enough it's the corporations that support mass immigration due to the simple economic fact that it increases the pool of potential workers therefore keeping the competition high and driving down labour costs via lower wages. Free market economics is generally a politically right leaning ideology whereas many conservatives and politically right of centre people will also support mass immigration, although they won't usually refer to it as *open borders* but instead espouse that immigrants are needed to fill the labour gap. Ann Coulter mentions this concept several times throughout her book titled *Adios America: The left's plan to turn our country into a third world hellhole* where she describes the corporate free market need for immigration as something that only benefits corporations (especially big corporations thus making them wealthy) because it supplies them with cheap labour. Corporate profits are sure to be higher so long as a large labour pool keeps potential workers accepting jobs at lower wages. Where this concept brakes down is when a country, such as Canada, essentially has open border policies, but still claims to have massive labour shortages and has corporations demanding even more immigration to fill this supposed labour shortage.[103] Considering that since 2016 tens of thousands of illegal immigrants have walked over the border from the United States into Canada to claim asylum and seek a better life, you would wonder why a province like Prince Edward Island has farmers who scream that they can't find workers to fill the labour void.

It would only stand to reason that if there are over 50 thousand illegal immigrants who trekked across the Canadian border from the United States in hopes of finding a better life[104], there certainly shouldn't be a labour shortage in any unskilled sector whatsoever. You would think that the government, open border advocates and social justice warriors would be rejoicing that there's plenty of work for these folks who only want a better life considering that employment is paramount in attaining success. The reason why employment isn't paramount for these illegal border crossers – despite that farmers in P.E.I. and elsewhere can't find enough workers – is because they are being housed, fed, clothed, cared for medically and much more at the decorum of the government making the entire scheme look great politically. Tens of thousands of illegal border crossers who broke the law by entering the

[102] http://www.migrantworkersrights.net/en/resources/the-exploitation-of-migrant-workers-in-canada--2

[103] https://business.financialpost.com/news/economy/canadian-businesses-message-ahead-of-the-election-we-need-immigrant-workers

[104] https://torontosun.com/opinion/columnists/lilley-trudeau-finally-closes-illegal-border-crossing

country unlawfully are now wards of the state and not even thought of as possible people who could be used to solve a major labour problem that corporations, and even governments, claim the country is suffering from despite an employment rate that is 10 percent or more in some parts of the country.[105]

The government is constantly pushing mass immigration on Canadians by proclaiming that there is a severe labour shortage in rural areas. Immigration minister Ahmed Hussen insists that small rural towns often have only one major employer and that that employer is desperate for workers and this desperation is having ill effects on those businesses. Hussen believes that Canada needs a major boost in immigration in order to offset this human deficit, and that immigration is the only way to solve the problem. Hussen describes these new immigrants as "settlers" who will benefit the economy and benefit the demographics of rural communities.[106] This use of the word "settler" is an interesting concept because it demonstrates how contemporary governments have the same social position as the European colonizers had when they implemented immigration policies that encouraged "settlers" to come to Canada. Early immigrant settlers were needed to farm and harvest the lands, which could be compared to what is taking place today by claiming that immigrants are needed for unskilled labour. At the end of the day we are once again reminded that immigration is an imperative necessity for Canadian society and once again it's the politicians that are endorsing this notion by ironically using the word "settler", which of course has its contemporary connotations with the white European occupation of Canada.

Now I challenge you to try and explain to an open border advocate, who declares that Canada needs immigrants because there's a labour shortage, that the only benefactor of this mass immigration is the corporations who want cheap labour and the government who wants to sell the idea of a contemporary colonialism. Furthermore, explain to an open border advocate, who argues that immigration is needed for cultural diversity and social enrichment, that today's immigration process is a mirrored reflection of what was implemented by white colonizers centuries ago. White settler immigration policies were all aimed at creating a labour force to enhance the social and financial needs of the corporate contingent of the colonizers along with creating a non-Indigenous society diverse with European cultures.[107] I highly doubt that it'll go over very well and I'm absolutely

---

[105] https://www150.statcan.gc.ca/n1/daily-quotidien/201204/dq201204a-eng.htm
[106] https://youtu.be/4ZZXLlO3wcY
[107] https://www.thecanadianencyclopedia.ca/en/article/immigration

positive that you'll be called the usual plethora of words implying bigot, racist, un-Canadian, xenophobe etc. Moreover, tell the next Indigenous person you see that Canada needs loads of more immigrants to fill the labour gap that corporations rave on about – corporations who are a direct product of white European colonialism – and see if the argument gets you any sympathy. Oh and don't forget to mention how there's a major need for greater cultural enrichment to go along with solving the corporate invented labour shortage: that would be the non-Indigenous cultural enrichment that requires the occupation of more lands and resources.

The cynicism with the issue of occupying Indigenous lands and resources by non-Indigenous people is that there now becomes common cause with other Indigenous lands that have been occupied by non-Indigenous people. One of the most notable instances of land and resources occupation is in the Israeli and Palestinian regions. This example of non-Indigenous occupation has created worldwide attention and has captured the hearts of social justice warriors in Canada who draw similarities between the white settler occupation in Canada and the Israeli occupation in the Palestinian region.

The Palestinians and Canada's Indigenous people: The hypocrisy of social justice Canadian style

The Palestinian cause is one of the most notable mainstream media fountainheads regarding oppression, colonization and stolen land while being a source for advocacy that demands immediate reparations for colonial injustices. The Palestinian issue of colonial injustices have morphed into an all out insistence demanding that the State of Israel return the occupied land that is said to be the rightful territory of the Palestinian people. The Palestinians claim to be the Indigenous people of the lands and that the lands were unlawfully and forcefully stolen from them by Israel and their supporting Western countries. The birthplace of the argument was highlighted after Great Britain and The United States supported the formation of the State of Israel in the region during the late 1940's. Without drudging back into the ancient history involving the Roman Empire, the Christian crusades or the Ottoman Empire, modern day Israel is disputed land and not officially recognized as a sovereign nation by many of its neighbouring countries. There is a general consensus among social justice advocates that the pertaining issues between Israel and Canada's Indigenous people are said to be very similar in many ways thereby creating a common cause.

Stolen land, European colonization and systemic oppression are something that the Palestinian and Indigenous people of Canada both endure. Many social justice advocates in Canada support the Palestinian cause by demanding boycotts of Israeli products and by demanding the outright removal of Israel from the geographical region. There has even been calls for the total destruction of the State of Israel by countries opposing its existence and the immediate return of all lands and resources to the Palestinians: the demand for the total destruction of Israel became infamous when Iran called for it to be wiped completely off the map. Otherwise, many people in Canada and elsewhere have aligned themselves with the Palestinian people and concur that they are victims of oppression, the very oppression that has its roots in colonialism. Just like in Canada today, colonialism doesn't necessarily have a direct relation to how the Indigenous people are being oppressed, but it does however occur do to a system that is colonial based. Israel is a country that may not necessarily have any direct colonial influence, but it is said to be a country that has a systemic structure specifically designed to oppress non-Jewish people such as the Palestinians. It can therefore be argued that the State of Israel is a structurally designed nation – much the same as Canada – that inherently systemically oppresses the Indigenous Palestinian people. A major commonality between Canada's Indigenous people and the Palestinian people is the theft of land and resources at the hands of powerfully backed authorities reminiscent of the past colonial occupiers in Canada.

After the Second World War, Jewish people who survived the holocaust began to migrate to the area that is now modern day Israel in hopes of establishing their own nation state. This migration is often referred to as the Jewish Zionist movement, which encourages Jewish people from all over the world to move to Israel.[108] The concept of mass migration and immigration into these disputed lands has been the focal point of contention between the Palestinian people and the neighbouring Muslim Arab countries. Current day Israel is situated on lands that are ancient, rich in history and historically significant to Christians, Jews and Muslims alike. Jewish Zionism however stands to ensure that the Jews are a strong, stable and formidable minority within the geographical region. For this reason, the State of Israel aligned itself with Great Britain and the United States all while having the blessing and official recognition of the United Nations as a country. Certainly the Holocaust caused the surviving Jewish people to desire strength through numbers and to ensure that a genocide like that never happens again. Safety through numbers can bring a sense of security, especially in a region where the minority group is literally surrounded by a majority group who greatly despises them. For this reason

---

[108] https://www.britannica.com/topic/Zionism

it is imperative that the minority group stand in complete solidarity with each other so as to ensure that there is total consensus relating to national unity. Total consensus can be hindered when sectorial conflicts arise such as the case with Orthodox Jews who believe that a Jewish state will only be created upon the return of the Messiah.[109] The return of the Messiah may be a long ways off, and meanwhile, there is a very strong movement advocating the return of Palestinian land to the Palestinian people.

It's one thing to see advocates in the Middle East demanding that Israel return land to the Palestinian people – who claim Indigenous status to such lands – but the complexity arises when advocates in Canada also demand that such lands be returned to the Palestinian people. Yes these Canadian activists feel virtuous in their foreign/overseas fight for the amelioration of an oppressed group of folks, but why don't these same activists demand that Canadian land seized under colonial rule be returned to the Canadian Indigenous people and that all non-Indigenous people be expelled? Exactly similar to what they demand should be done in Israel. This begins the oxymoronic segment of *social justice Canadian style* where several different advocate groups all have a common cause: a common cause of fighting for an oppressed group of people who claim their land was stolen by some type of colonial power.

When examining the various advocate groups who plead the case on behalf of Palestinians, it's not so much the commonalities that should be critiqued, but it's the contradictions that should be highlighted instead. Every social justice advocate who claims that Israel stole Palestinian land will also tell you that the European colonizers done the exact same thing to Canada's Indigenous people. Now if you're on the side of the "stolen land" issue, then yes you must concur that there is indeed the perception of stolen land in one-way-or-another. Viewing the issue through the lens of oppressor versus oppressed, it's absolutely irrefutable that there was stolen land in one-way-or-another. The irony is that while these social justice advocates claim that the stolen Palestinian land should be returned to the rightful owners, they are just as willing to champion the influx of more non-Indigenous people into Canada simply due to their support for open borders through multiculturalism. The cynical nature of social justice advocates, who don't see an issue with millions of non-Indigenous people immigrating to Canada under current multiculturalism as a form of contemporary colonialism, is what makes the Palestinian land issue so baffling. If there is a fight for a cause to rid a land of the non-Indigenous people and a return of the land to the Indigenous people then how

---

can there be support for the immigration of massive amounts of non-Indigenous people into Indigenous lands as there currently is in Canada?

Making it a race issue makes it interesting, noticeable and fashionable

Drawing a comparison between the Palestinian cause and the cause of the Canadian Indigenous people is only a social justice token that is used by advocates where they can extrapolate something that they deem as a *racial oppression*. The issue of race is always a convenient way to arouse an emotional response and to inflict guilt on those who either don't agree with it or who may simply ignore it because they may not be too concerned about the issue. Injecting race into the issue is a sure-fire way to capture the attention of those people who are passionate about racial injustices and those who love a juicy news story.

Take for example the idle no more movement that swept canada a few years back creating momentum in many cities by calling for the amelioration of Canada's Indigenous people who have been victimized by colonialism. The Palestinian cause has been used on a comparable level by aligning itself with Canada's Indigenous people and how they have suffered at the hands of colonialism. Non-Indigenous social justice warriors are quick to capitalize on the misfortunes that the Indigenous people have suffered despite these social justice warriors being a product of the colonial immigration system themselves and by not renouncing their own colonial roots and citizenship. The Canadian Palestinian Association have aligned themselves with the Idle no more movement by proclaiming that they too are victims of colonialism just the same as Canada's Indigenous people are.[110] The fact that the CPA have chosen to align themselves with the Indigenous people of Canada could be something of a subjective interpretation. From one angle it could be perceived that Canada's Indigenous people have thrown themselves at the CPA and declaring that the Palestinian people have suffered just the same as them. It could also be perceived that it's the CPA who have sought out the Indigenous people and offered to be an unlikely ally. If indeed Canada's Indigenous people sought out the Palestinians in order to bolster their cause then why use an immigrant group of people who were permitted to settle in Canada under multiculturalism resembling colonial immigration policies? If it was the CPA who sought out Canada's Indigenous people as an ally then wouldn't this be a form of racial opportunism designed as an appeal to emotion? After all, you can bet that the members of the CPA and their supporters are all benefactors of a generous immigration system that allowed them to settle in Canada in the first place and it's

---

[110] https://www.haaretz.com/.premium-canadian-natives-palestinians-rally-for-colonized-1.5227384

very unlikely that they would leave Canada as an act of solidarity due to it being on the stolen lands of the Indigenous people.

Heather Milton Lightening describes the Palestinians residing within Israel as Indigenous people and compares their struggle to the Canadian Indigenous people and how they are displaced by colonialism. Lightening also believes that Canada's Indigenous people have a responsibility to help the Palestinian people and that the Boycott, Divestment and Sanctions (BDS) against Israel is a worthy cause.[111] Championing the BDS movement as a means to redress the wrongs of European colonialism creates a situation where Indigenous people are now reduced to racial tokens. The fact that Israel had nothing to do with the theft of Indigenous lands, residential schools, the sixties scoop or any other travesty committed by colonial forces in Canada only devalues the suffering actually occurred by Canada's Indigenous people. Instead Heather Milton Lightening is selling out the suffering that did occur to an unrelated social cause thereby allowing her people to be tokenized by a contemporary group of immigrants who have chosen to settle in Canada due to open immigration policies and multiculturalism. Watching the video where Heather Milton Lightening explains that Indigenous people have suffered in many of the same ways as the Palestinians have and how they all have been oppressed by colonial forces is rather humours when the video shows the audience. The audience consists of mostly white folks and a few Muslim looking women in the front row sporting their hijabs who are all benefactors of the colonial forces that opened up Canada to non-Indigenous settlers in the first place. The only difference is that the colonial forces of the past are all but gone and have been replaced with the contemporary version of colonialism through multiculturalism and a government that believes open borders are what's best for Canada and its citizens.

This is a prime example of how modern governments use colonial policies that are disguised as modern initiatives and which they claim will benefit everyone. The result is a large group of non-Indigenous people who are all privileged by past colonialism and who are completely fooled into believing that the modern government initiatives of immigration don't resemble past colonial policies that admitted millions of non-Indigenous people into the country. What we end up witnessing is white folks and their new immigrant counterparts all advocating for what they think is Indigenous rights not knowing that they are actually being used by politicians as tokens for the contemporary colonialism being peddled under the name of multiculturalism. Politicians stand to gain tremendously from groups of

---

[111] https://youtu.be/RF-rCYn6yil

people who claim that they are oppressed and need to align themselves with others who also feel that they've been oppressed. This creates a social cause that in turn creates a voting bloc and allows politicians to capture and secure a larger portion of the total voting populace. It also allows politicians to convince these useful idiots that the modern immigration policies are somehow better than the past colonial policies; the past colonial policies that are being used as an explanation for modern day oppression. Contemporary immigration policies that politicians peddle have allowed millions more non-Indigenous people into the country than past colonial policies ever have and is a fact that these useful idiots conveniently choose to ignore.

The social justice advocacy of Heather Milton Lightening is not limited only to her, but also a plethora of other people who espouse the same concepts as she does. Aligning the Palestinian cause with Canada's Indigenous people's struggle to overcome what they describe as the generational victimization of colonialism works as a convenient argument that blames white settler nations and their laws, which have provided so many people with numerous freedoms; including the freedom to condemn, criticize and display complete contempt towards the country of Canada. Case in point is a video from the Rebel Media where David Menzies interviewed a Canadian Muslim at a pro-Palestinian rally who strongly advocates the replacement of Canadian law with Islamic law so that gays can be killed.[112] This person advocating Muslim Islamic law goes as far as to suggest that Canada is on stolen land from the Native Canadians while also further suggesting that Canadians should respect other people's cultures and religions accordingly. The irony is that this pro-Palestinian Muslim man forgets – or simply doesn't know – that members from his own religious community have proudly and openly aligned themselves with the cause of Canada's Indigenous people while somehow forgetting that Canada's Indigenous people have historically supported gays. Two spirited Indigenous people have always been welcomed in Aboriginal communities and have never been persecuted, unlike what the aforementioned Muslim man calls for. Two spirited Indigenous people are defined as those who are gay or who identify as the gender they feel they are and are recognized as important members of society.[113] In fact the "2" in the acronym LGBTQ2+ specifically refers to the two spirited Indigenous folks who are gay or gender fluid/binary or who wish to identify as such. The concept of gender identity and identification has created a great deal of controversy due to the fact that a person may simply identify as the

---

[112] https://www.therebel.media/toronto-muslim-al-quds-day-rally-executing-gays-part-of-sharia-law-replacement-birth-rates
[113] https://lgbtqhealth.ca/community/two-spirit.php

opposite sex and that this decision is to be accepted by everyone without question or debate.

To question or attempt to debate this gender identification is completely frowned upon and has actually cost those who've done so a great price. Professor Jordan Peterson of the University of Toronto has been shunned by the vast majority of his professional colleagues because he refused to agree with mandated requirements to use gender pronouns that people wish to identify as. Peterson has created a great deal of contention within academia and the mainstream media regarding his stance, prompting him from backing down, thereby standing firm on his position. Even students who cite Peterson have been scorned; such as the case with student Lindsay Shepard who faced disciplinary action from her university's officials after she was accused of creating an uncomfortable and potentially dangerous environment when showing a video clip of Peterson. How social justice advocates justify aligning themselves with a cause that holds contradictory foundational elements sleep at night is beyond anything that I could imagine: especially a contradiction such as homosexuality, Indigenous people's and Palestinian rights and how the religion of Islam holds many ultra-conservative tenets. Nevertheless, there is an ironic coalition between the religion of Islam and the Indigenous people of Canada that is eternized through the social and political cause of the Palestinian people and the fight against colonialism and the white settler societies it created.

Strength through numbers

Aligning a social cause with those who claim to have been oppressed in a similar fashion can be a strong way to gather collective social and political capital and garner greater attention. But there should obviously be a common theme that is able to justify a coalition between two or more groups. Employment unions often do this by finding alliances between different groups of workers who have similar occupational environments or who have similar occupational roles. Perhaps using the analogy of a collective groups of folks, such as a union, is kind of a misnomer into itself, but the point is that even though there are two or more different groups, their social cause will be clearly similar and not conflict in any way. Using the example of a social cause that requires the advocacy of a union that is fighting for the protection of workers rights would clearly not involve the advocacy of the employer or corporate entity that is alleged to be oppressing the worker: unless of course it was to meet with the employer or corporate entity for the purpose of collective bargaining or to hold discussions to resolve the situation. You would never expect to hear a union claim that the corporate owners and employers are also suffering too and must be acknowledged as fellow victims of workplace oppression and exploitation and that there is a commonality between the workers and owners. Well that's exactly what is happening between the Palestinian and the Indigenous people who somehow think that their social cause is related. The peculiarity is fully captured when social justice warriors like Joshua Blakeney espouse that Canada's Indigenous people are essentially Canada's Palestinian people and that the oppression from the government must stop.[114] Suggesting that an identifiable group is subjected to inherent racism by virtue of the fact that they have suffered land loss and resource theft, which automatically places them in a special category resembling a social intersectional hierarchy, raises more questions than it provides answers. Blakeney is a prime example of a person who uses pseudo intellectual arguments based on emotions while strongly possessing a racial element. An argument like this solely suggests that it's the systemic and institutional racism stemming, from colonialism, that causes the racial inequalities that result in the pronouncement of oppression and creates a default condition where the two separate groups are now aligned as one. Questions then arise as to how can two different groups who have different cultural, religious, social and political viewpoints claim to be one group aimed at fighting for a common cause? Without drawing on previous points, consideration should be given to how the two spirited sexual concept has been poached by the mainstream LGBT community by making it a major point of commemoration of social equality, but in doing this they fail to realize how this notion wouldn't even remotely be considered within the Palestinian nation due to their ultra conservative religious beliefs.

Blakeney further suggests that Canada's Indigenous people be given autonomy, self-determination and be allowed to make their own mistakes all while he subjectively compares them to the people of Palestine. His subjective measurement of Canada's Indigenous people being implicitly equalized to the Palestinians, in terms of social oppression, is laughable at best and should be given as much credence as as soup-sandwich. How can someone who is neither Indigenous or Palestinian and who has probably never suffered any of the social disadvantages that either group claims to suffer even fathom the concept of comparing the two and then claiming to be a representative of the two? This once again clearly demonstrates the dangerous white men concept. This is what makes the entire idea of social justice advocating a complete farce while disintegrating what injustices there may be. On top of this, there is the complete idiocy when Canada accepts the very immigrants – who claim to be refugees – from the Palestinian region and watch them align with the Indigenous people and then slander Canada as an oppressive colonial society that is full of racism. It's one thing to see the one way

---

[114] https://youtu.be/p05I5BltzvQ

immigration flow into Canada because it's an open, inclusive, welcoming, tolerant and a multicultural nation, but it's ironic that we don't see a mass exodus of people from Canada in order to restore it to its original Indigenous roots. Why isn't there a mass exodus of social justice warriors leaving Canada and moving to the Palestinian region to fight for their equality? Instead it's much easier to paint Canada as a white settler society that is inherently racist and oppressive despite the fact that it's Canada that's the first choice for all the refugees and immigrants to come to when they want freedom and a better quality of life. It's also because Canadians are welcoming and want nothing more than to make the world a better place and Canada's Indigenous people are eager to have allies in their social cause. Allies, such as the Palestinians, can easily incite the necessary emotions from generous Canadians who want to make the world a better place and who want to show the world what a diverse nation is and what it represents.

Chapter 11: Return the land back to the Indigenous people. The white folks feel guilty.

> *When the equality advocates, who dream of correcting an oppressive white society, only see the option of mass immigration through multiculturalism as a solution to racial inequities, they unknowingly continue the process of further colonization of Indigenous lands without any trepidation whatsoever.*

The term *white guilt* is often thrown around in such a manner that it becomes an overkill, and most people that the term applies to don't have any real idea of what it actually means. They do however respond to the term as if they are compelled to, thus acting accordingly, by affirming that they feel a certain social guilt due to a form of racial privilege granted to white folks through colonialism. In relation to multiculturalism and Indigenous people, the guilty white person will unquestionably endorse multiculturalism, while at the same time, acknowledging the injustices of past colonialism itself while holding the supposition that Canada is on stolen lands. This creates an obvious contradiction whereas the guilty white person (usually politically liberal/left-leaning) unwittingly endorses further colonialism against the Indigenous people by championing open borders, cultural and ethnic diversity as being a core component of contemporary society. Phrases like, "we owe it to less fortunate people who we've hurt through foreign policies" or " we have an obligation to help those people" or " it's our responsibility because of how we oppressed those not like us", is an all to common parlance of the guilty white people. Although these statements are in quotations, and not directly cited, they can easily be understood from an anecdotal perspective when one simply hears the cries of the white folks on the political left who evangelize that racial equality will only be achieved through cultural and racial diversity. Buying into the concept that multiculturalism is about making society more racially diverse and that this racial diversity will reduce racism isn't the right course of action that should be taken.

Reducing racism is not as simple as injecting large numbers of non-white people into a society that was colonized by whites in hopes of racially foreshortening white people. When the equality advocates, who dream of correcting an oppressive white society, only see the option of mass immigration through multiculturalism as a solution to racial inequities, they unknowingly continue the process of further colonizing Indigenous lands without any trepidation whatsoever. Doing this entitles them to a sense of achievement and a sense of reconciliation and social justice therefore suppressing their white guilt and white privilege that they proudly acknowledge having. While the guilty white person marches in solidarity with the multiculturalists, who are trumpeting acclaimed solutions to society's racial misgivings, they also ignorantly proclaim their own hypocrisy without even knowing it. It is very unlikely that one of those inglorious social justice warriors would ever open up a room or space in their own home for a so-called refugee or financially strapped immigrant yet alone open their home to an Indigenous person who has suffered due to colonialism. Genuine reconciliation is a notion that social justice warriors could not define yet alone fathom. Reconciliation, in a pure genuine form, essentially can't be defined without referring to the usual political rhetoric that spews notions of talks, funding for programs all aimed at addressing past injustices and moving towards a post-colonial state. Yes past and present governments have initiated inquiries into the effects of colonialism, but there has never been any concrete solution that has occurred as a result of such inquiries other than basic bullet point recommendations that usually involve increasing government funding for the Indigenous people. The term reconciliation is sadly a misnomer that only creates the illusion that white people are helping to ameliorate the injustices that colonialism perpetuated against the Indigenous people. It's a political buzzword that politicians, academics, intellectuals and the mainstream media emits in order to sound like virtuous people who are championing for the underdog. What true reconciliation looks like would be the actual return of all lands and all resources to the Indigenous people as opposed to constantly talking about how all the past colonial injustices have created an inherently oppressive society that is still active today. Again, you would be hard pressed to find anyone willing to simply give up their land in the name of reconciliation but you'll hear endless talk from guilty white people about how the said lands still belongs to the Indigenous people while they praise multiculturalism and the mass immigration that goes with it.

Individual reconciliation

British Columbia farmer Kenneth Linde is a notable exception to the usual *reconciliation* hypocrisy – that social justice warriors spew relating to the stolen land concept – after he surrendered part of his ranch to his nearby Indigenous community who he felt had an inherent right to that land. In an act of individual reconciliation, Linde decided to give back half his land, amounting to 130 hectares, to the Esk'etemc First Nations.[115] Linde's family operated a sawmill in the community for decades and had employed many Indigenous people who belonged to the Esk'etemc community. The extremely noble act of Kenneth Linde is certainly a rarity and one of a kind that surprisingly never made the headline news as story of the year. One would think that Linde would've been featured on the cover of a major Canadian magazine – as opposed to a convicted terrorist who killed a U.S. soldier in Afghanistan and blinded another and who's family had strong links to Al-Queda. Unfortunately though the story of Kenneth Linde doesn't fit the political narrative of diversity as strength and it definitely doesn't fit the narrative of how contemporary Canada is defined as a multicultural society that was built by immigrants on stolen land. The story of Linde would also shame the virtue signallers who spew massive amounts of rhetoric about how evil and how greedy white Canadians are and how they are responsible for the decay of the Indigenous people's connection to their land do to colonialism. Kenneth Linde's story would also further shame the virtue signalling social justice warriors as to their own inability to step up to the plate and attempt an act of personal reconciliation. The driving factor in preventing the guilty white people from stepping up to the plate goes far beyond their inadequate contributions of simply calling people racist and then accusing then of white privilege, it actually stems from their own racial privilege that they fail to recognize. According to author Robin DiAngelo, the thing preventing white people from seeing the errors of their guilty ways can be described as lacking racial stamina to engage in difficult racial

---

[115] https://www.cbc.ca/radio/asithappens/as-it-happens-friday-edition-1.4112585/reconciliation-in-its-best-form-b-c-rancher-gives-land-back-to-his-first-nation-neighbours-1.4112589

conversations.[116] This concept suggests that white folks may take comfort in being isolated from people of colour and that this social buffer can blind them to the reality outside their protective and privileged shell. In other words, white people relish in the segregation that multiculturalism offers due to the ethnic enclaves that inherently result from it. The ethnic enclaves of the Indigenous people come by way of federal mandated reserves that were assigned through colonialism isolating white folks and excusing them of any responsibility for occupying Indigenous lands. Now when a white person, such as Kenneth Linde, actually steps up to the plate and does something to remedy the past injustices committed by whites, the media, academics, social science intellectuals and politicians all remain completely silent – with the exception of the cited CBC article about Kenneth Linde. White folks can simply sit back in their racial comfort zone, where they fully support mass immigration, via multiculturalism, and act as advocates on behalf of the oppressed Indigenous people and proclaim that it's white people and colonialism that's to blame for everything.

The silence from the media, government, intellectuals and social justice warriors about the Kenneth Linde situation could definitely be a result of what DiAngelo refers to as white fragility due to the fact that it was virtually ignored by those who always claim to fight for the Indigenous people. The silence could have also resulted from the fact that Kenneth Linde's son filed a legal claim to prevent the transfer of land to the Esk'etemc community and that the courts ruled in favour of Linde junior and halted the land transfer.[117] Even that fact that the courts revoked the transfer of land from Kenneth Linde to the Esk'etemc community should have been enough to stir up the proverbial reactions from the social justice warrior types as a failure of the colonial legal establishment and structure. Nevertheless, the silence is deafening but certainly questionable. If politicians were truly inspired by Kenneth Linde's upstanding act of individual reconciliation and followed suit, this might encourage other white folks to do the same thus making individual reconciliation an encouraging and noble action while adding an element of personal responsibility toward racial amelioration. It would be highly unlikely that a politician would ever surrender their own property yet alone encourage others to do the same, but they sure would promise Indigenous people that the government

---

[116] https://www.newyorker.com/books/page-turner/a-sociologist-examines-the-white-fragility-that-prevents-white-americans-from-confronting-racism

[117] http://sabeyrule.ca/wp-content/uploads/2019/09/Linde-v-Linde-2019-BCSC-1586.pdf

will take care of them if elected. Politicians can promise inquiries, funding for research, set up committees and increase the bureaucracies relating to Indigenous people's issues, but they would never surrender their own land or encourage others to do so. The mainstream media, intellectuals or social justice warriors would never take an interest in pushing the narrative of individual reconciliation because it would place the onus on the every day person to step up and surrender what assets they have acquired themselves. Blaming the colonial establishment is what helps make stories newsworthy; by creating a victim and a villain: the villain being the colonial establishment and the Indigenous people as the victim. Any form of individual reconciliation, that defeats the entire mainstream political narrative, is discouraged because it places an onus on the individual to reconcile thereby forcing intellectuals, politicians and social justice warriors out of their collective shell of protection that multiculturalism provides.

Why the mainstream media, politicians and social justice warriors didn't jump on the fact that the courts reversed the heroic act of personal reconciliation by Kenneth Linde is truly perplexing. Reading the B.C.'s court decision and playing the devil's advocate, it could be surmised that Kenneth Linde only gave the portion of his land to the Indigenous people in order to spite his son and daughter in-law. For this reason maybe the media, politicians and social justice warriors alike decided that it would be best to ignore the story and continue on their usual path of strength through diversity and that multiculturalism is the way to achieve such strength and diversity.

The act of individual reconciliation by returning personal land to the Indigenous people is something that has not caught on in Canada, but British Columbia did have another case of personal reconciliation when Penelope Harris graciously gifted two parcels of her land to the Lheidli T'enneh First Nations. Harris stated that she believed that it was their land in the first place and that they would be better stewards of it.[118] Just as with the Kenneth Linde story, there was very little media coverage of this personal act of reconciliation despite the fact that Harris believed that her actions would help heal the injustices that the Indigenous people have endured. The acts of Linde and Harris could be viewed as personal examples of *paying it forward* and how the individual who benefited from the colonial structure has decided to check their privilege and acknowledge their inherent position of racial power in a white settler society. Perhaps the media was too

---

[118] https://www.princegeorgecitizen.com/news/local-news/landowner-donates-land-to-lheidli-t-enneh-1.23795039

scared to capitalize on a story of personal reconciliation due to possible peculiarities in the case of Harris where prior to gifting her land to the Lheidli T'enneh First Nations she was unsuccessful in her bid to sell it. Harris told the local news that the Western Canadian Wilderness Committee suggested that she give the land to local First Nations [119] after years of owning it and never using it. Just as with the Linde case where it might appear that he only gave the land to the Indigenous people in order to spite his son, it's possible that there could have been criticism that Harris only wanted to get rid of the land and the possible burden it included by way of property taxes and or income tax issues of some sort. Nevertheless, the criticisms in both cases could have been overshadowed with the usual rebuttals and accusations of racism when someone questioned the sincerity or motives of the gift giving. After all, the gift giving by surrendering personal land to the Indigenous people is definitely an unprecedented event and creates an angle that sets a new standard of personal responsibility for the white person. This new angle could suggest that the white person must truly confront their privilege and it's certainly amazing that the social justice warriors never captured this concept and ran with it by demanding that whites return their land back to the Indigenous people.

Natural resources

Debates over Indigenous land claims often occur when there are issues relating to crown land. Oil pipelines in Western Canada are often a contentious issue when oil companies want to build or expand their operations on or near crown land or First Nations territory. Transporting natural resources, such as petroleum products, will certainly attract the attention of the concerned white folks who are usually the first ones to disapprove citing the best interest of the Indigenous people. Once again, we see how the white folks are acting as the advocates for the Indigenous people by claiming that their land must be protected from the ever encroaching white powers. Interestingly enough, but not surprising, white folks take the front stage in the protest against natural gas pipelines in British Colombia when roads were blocked, government buildings blockaded and general protests were held all over Canada in solidarity with the Indigenous people who are allegedly impacted. All to often these white folks have virtually no idea what they are really protesting – other than the fact that they believe they are supporting the Indigenous people – but

---

[119] https://www.princegeorgematters.com/local-news/photos-for-the-first-time-ever-a-private-landowner-gifts-land-back-to-lheidli-tenneh-1379968

nevertheless these white folks feel obligated to speak and advocate a social cause that grants them moral virtue.[120]

In Prince Edward Island there was an ongoing matter of the Mill River resort, land that was purchased by Dan McDougall from the province: property that is said to be the inherent land of the Mi'kmaq First Nations who were the original inhabitants of P.E.I. The Mi'kmaq people disputed the sale due to a lack of consultation that was prescribed pursuant to a Supreme Court of Canada ruling in 2005. This SCC ruling specified that any crown lands to be sold must undergo a reasonable process of consultation when there may be a First Nations group impacted by the sale. The Mi'kmaq people of P.E.I. argued that the sale could cause adverse effects to them and that the sale should be halted. The courts however decided otherwise by stating that the Mi'kmaq people failed to prove their case despite the fact that they planned to bring an Aboriginal land claim for the entire province of P.E.I.[121]

Land claims from the Mi'kmaq people on P.E.I. are nothing new. Chief Brian Francis said that the entire island belongs to the Mi'kmaq people and that the Mi'kmaq have never ceded any land to the first European settlers; while at the same time, Chief Matilda Ramjattan analogies the European occupation to that of inviting your in-laws or neighbours coming over and then having them take over your home.[122] Claiming the entire province of Prince Edward Island as Mi'kmaq territory is also backed up by the fact that the Mi'kmaq have been on the island for over ten thousand years thus giving them an inherent right to the land and it's resources.

The Mill River resort sale touched some nerves in the white settler community when professor Peter McKenna of the University of Prince Edward Island wrote and opinion piece in the Charlottetown Guardian stating his disgust for the court decision. McKenna asserted the fact that the Mi'kmaq people have been on P.E.I. for over 12 thousand years and that the court's decision was a reflection of ever present colonialism.[123] In response to professor McKenna, I wrote a letter to the editor in the Charlottetown Guardian acknowledging the damage of colonialism while stating that contemporary immigration is allowing large amounts of new

---

[120] https://youtu.be/Rh59EXGmRXc

[121] https://www.cbc.ca/news/canada/prince-edward-island/pei-mikmaq-mill-river-appeal-dismissed-nov-2019-1.5358369

[122] https://www.cbc.ca/news/canada/prince-edward-island/pei-mi-kmaq-native-aboriginal-land-rights-1.4008521

[123] Charlottetown Guardian. November, 25 2019

settlers into Canada through various governmental programs that essentially amounts to contemporary colonialism.[124] Professor McKenna's heart is in the right place regarding the *best interest* of P.E.I.'s Indigenous people and he does make a valid point relating to the harm that colonialism has caused them due to the loss of their land. This *best interest* of the Indigenous people however appears to be opportunistic and leaning heavily on the side of pure virtue signalling thus demonstrating the point of how white people can talk a good talk. When the issue of contemporary immigration and the massive amounts of new settlers that it produces are conveniently ignored in order to force a one sided agenda, the *best interest* aspect becomes self-serving falling into the dangerous white people category. If social justice warriors truly believe that P.E.I. still belongs to the Mi'kmaq then they should be advocating an end to further colonization through immigration, encourage the personal surrender of unneeded and unnecessary land and demand the return of all crown land back to the Indigenous people. They should then perhaps demand the expelling of all non-Indigenous people out of the entire province so that it is returned to the Mi'kmaq people. Unfortunately it's much easier for white folks to armchair quarterback and critique modern society as one that is oppressive and racist while completely ignoring how multiculturalism is the driving factor for immigration levels that have far surpassed initial European colonialism.

In Prince Edward Island there are still ongoing issues of land reconciliation between First Nations and the government, but because the Mi'kmaq people have never ceded the province to colonial settlers, there remains a serious question: is there any clout to the claim that P.E.I. actually belongs to the Indigenous people without an official treaty or agreement? Since the inception of Section 35(1) of the 1982 Constitution, all treaties have been legally recognized as binding and enforceable and this is the working point that the Mi'kmaq people rely on.[125] This lack of clarity shows that colonialism is still ever-present and that merely staking a claim to something, such as land, is completely futile. Twelve thousand years of previous occupation is a strong argument of the Mi'kmaq people but it holds no legal influence whatsoever in the contemporary courts of law. It is however the strongest argument for a white person who feels that they must display a courageous act of self indignation against the white settler society and the harm it has caused towards the Indigenous people, but it's unfortunately not enough to win

---

[124] https://www.pressreader.com/canada/the-guardian-charlottetown/20191207/281702616587476

[125] https://www.princeedwardisland.ca/en/information/executive-council-office/understanding-indigenous-matters

a land claim case. Unless the white settler folks step up and take the matter of reconciliation into their own hands in the way Kenneth Linde and Penelope Harris did, there's not much hope for any legally enforceable means for the Mi'kmaq people to acquire their departed lands on P.E.I. Further to this there is even less hope for Indigenous people to reacquire their lands elsewhere in Canada so long as immigration through multiculturalism continues thereby increasing the non-Indigenous settler population even more. These are sadly the key factors that will ensure continued colonialism and ensure that white European power and ideology continues to oppress the Indigenous people through immigration and ensure that the term *post-colonialism* remains a word influenced by political semantics.

Chapter 12: Political opposition of multiculturalism past and present.

> *All the support for multiculturalism is given without any regard to the Indigenous people as stakeholders and without the consideration of how the unfettered implementation of more non-Indigenous people, into an already colonized society, would impact Indigenous people even further.*

Initial opposition to federally instituted multiculturalism didn't come without resistance citing that Canada would essentially lose its British and French based culture and identity. When Prime Minister Pierre Trudeau christened the concept of multiculturalism as a means to insert ethnic diversity into Canadian society, he was confronted with opposition. Politicians of that era clearly outlined that Canada had its historical roots in British and French culture and that imposing or mandating a program of legislated multiculturalism would put those roots in peril. Time would however show that these fears of losing a national identity were essentially frivolous due to political yielding that saw little opposition to a federally mandated program of official multiculturalism. 1971 saw the liberals, under Pierre Trudeau, declare Canada as the first multicultural country in the world and 1988 saw Brian Mulroney's Progressive Conservatives pass the official multiculturalism act thereby confirming Canada as a country open to anyone who would increase the ethnic diversity. Since then, nearly every politician has embraced multiculturalism and has promised ever increasing numbers of immigrants will be given Canadian citizenship and that Canada's identity is rooted in diverse immigration and not necessarily British or French roots alone. Today those who oppose multiculturalism are simply deemed as racist regardless of their reasons and regardless of how they may justify their reasons, but this does not mean that there haven't been politicians opposed to it and who have expressed their opposition openly. Maxime Bernier is one such notable Canadian politician who has openly stated that multiculturalism is a failure and that mass immigration is doing more harm than good. He has also been vocal about how multiculturalism is eroding the Canadian culture which he believes is rooted in the historical English and French elements of society. These viewpoints have earned Bernier the usual title of racist and a xenophobe despite the fact that he is willing to debate politicians and regular folks about the matter. Bernier was initially disqualified as a participant in the Canadian electoral debates on the grounds that he was racist and xenophobic and that his party (The People's Party of Canada) was not a legitimate mainstream party. Those who wanted to block Bernier suggested that his party was merely a fringe political concept that only a small minority of people belonged to and supported and that it didn't reflect Canadian values.[126]

These Canadian values are the contemporary concept of diversity as strength, open borders, mass immigration and hasty refugee intakes that all fall under the guise of multiculturalism and that it was immigration as a sole factor that built the country from the ground up. All the support for multiculturalism is given without any regard to the Indigenous people as stakeholders and without the consideration of how the unfettered implementation of more non-Indigenous people, into an already colonized society, would impact Indigenous people even further. Bernier and his Canadian People's Party has a mandate to limit immigration to number significantly lower than the current Liberal government. These immigration reforms would include a reclassification of what a refugee is and would also include stricter enforcement at the borders thus preventing migrants seeking asylum from the United States.[127] This is clearly in direct contrast to the current Liberal government's approach that has allowed and encouraged tens of thousands of U.S. migrants to illegally walk into Canada between official ports of entry. Again this approach of Maxime Bernier's has been met with accusations of racism and accusations that he is in defiance of Canadian values. Even those people who are on the right leaning side of the political spectrum contend that Bernier is portraying racist behaviour and suggest that his party is unfit to represent Canadians and that it will attract racists.[128] Bernier and his party completely

---

[126] https://www.cbc.ca/news/politics/leaders-debate-commission-maxime-bernier-out-1.5244287

[127] https://www.ctvnews.ca/mobile/politics/bernier-promises-to-build-border-fences-if-elected-pm-1.4522382

flopped in the 2019 federal election which saw Justin Trudeau win a minority government. Even though Bernier holds the belief that mass immigration is not good for Canada and traditional Canadian values, he grossly fell short of capturing the position that mass immigration, whether it be via multiculturalism or otherwise, would only amount to another form of colonialism thereby creating even further injustices for Indigenous people. Instead he was portrayed as being racist and un-Canadian and someone who was not fit for political office. This once again demonstrates that contemporary politics must include the concept of large scale immigration and any opposition to it is not worthy of a debate, but only worthy of accusations of racism irrespective of how such mass immigration may impact Indigenous people.

Should common sense suggest that the more people there are the more land and resources that will be required to accommodate them?

The common term that is used in academia and among the educated elites to describe a post-colonial society, such as Canada, is *white settler society*. This term rings with explanations and apologies that describe and acknowledge how Canada was the land of the Indigenous people and how it was taken, pillaged of its resources and then occupied by white Europeans.[129] The *white settler* concept was instrumental in establishing the racial hierarchy that saw the whites at the top of the social pecking order while being pivotal in instituting modern day whiteness as a major component of a post-colonial society. The term white settler refers exclusively to the white Europeans and their descendants who were and are the occupying forces of the colonized lands. This term ostensibly does not include any contemporary people who stem from immigration programs initiated by governments – whether it be multiculturalism, refugee intakes, humanitarian immigration, family reunification or any other host of immigration schemes that politicians dream up in order to appear morally correct. White settler society specifically means the mass immigration of white Europeans who were central in creating the Canadian society that oppressed and continues to oppress the Indigenous people to this day. To insinuate that contemporary new comers to Canada and their off-spring are settlers is something that is sure to be met with many objections. During the initial opposition of official multiculturalism, the

---

[128] https://www.cbc.ca/news/politics/bernier-peoples-party-canada-1.4823647

[129] https://www.encyclopedia.com/social-sciences/encyclopedias-almanacs-transcripts-and-maps/white-settler-society

opposing politicians never suggested that it would further colonize the Indigenous people with even more settlers, but instead they focused on how it would destroy the Europeanization of Canada and the whiteness it established. In the end, those opposed to multiculturalism capitulated and caved into it without a fight and without offering any advocacy on behalf of Indigenous people due to the further increase in immigration that would create more demand for land and resources.

Continued victimization of Indigenous people by past colonialism

There is a school of thought that Indigenous people are still being victimized by the antiquated results of colonialism along with a strong element of contention suggesting reparations in the form of open access to lands for, whatever purpose, is one solution. The purpose of making more land available to Indigenous people could be for housing, business or traditional uses. Metaphorically having the *discussion* as to how to fix the negative impacts of colonialism and suggesting that Indigenous people should be able to use any piece of land as they so desire will certainly get you an A on your university paper but that's as far as it will go. The reality is that those very people (most of whom aren't Indigenous) who advocate the return of lands to the Indigenous people, and the unfettered use of it, would never give their own lands back as a gesture of regret for past colonial injustices. Conservative commentator Michael J. Knowles stated this during a university discussion on colonialism by saying that those who attack the American colonial establishment for occupying land once owned by the Indigenous people also occupy the same land as the colonialist and have no intentions of leaving or returning the land.[130] Knowles makes a good point about how privileged these university students are and the potential power they have to enact social change. Instead the social justice warriors merely parade around in an apparent cloak of virtue preaching harmony and proclaiming that it must be everyone else who should pay reparations or who must reconcile past deeds. It's very true that the younger generation of adults in universities have the ability to critique society and identify antiquated aspects that should be changed in order to make society a better place. Sadly enough, these very privileged students only critique the social elements that fit their agenda of oppressor versus oppressed because it's what post-secondary institutions usually encourage: and besides it's an easy A on the good ole term paper. At the end of the day, absolutely none of these students, professors or social justice warrior types would ever give up their land or property or return to

---

[130] https://youtu.be/uaMqzlo5KWY

their ancestral countries, yet alone even open their doors to an Indigenous person needing a home or a place to stay. The same can be said for those open border advocates who proclaim that multiculturalism is necessary as it defines Canada's identity and is necessary to ensure a form of social strength: they would also never open their own doors to new immigrants, but think that the idea of opening the national borders is completely fine.

Open border advocates and social justice warriors conveniently ignore the fact that immigration is the same as settlement, but have absolutely no reservations telling us how Canada is a white settler society. Blogger and businessman Cory Morgan alluded to this scenario when he Tweeted: *Step back & look at this "settler" bullshit label that some are giving to all non-native Canadians. How would it look if white Canadians called the children of all non-white immigrant Canadians "settlers" even if they were born here. Its gross racism in both cases.*[131] Attacking colonialism is an easy undertaking when someone wants to critique modern society and demand social change that will ensure egalitarianism. But why isn't colonialism attacked and critiqued beginning with how the supposition that Canada was, and is, a country of immigrants who are said to be the ones credited with building the country and how immigration is still needed today to maintain the country? By believing that Canada is a country of immigrants and that immigration must continue in order for Canada to continue as a successful nation, you inadvertently make the entire notion of contemporary immigration an obvious fallacy. The obvious fallacy is by failing to consider how immigration is what the past colonial powers used to occupy Indigenous lands and to create their ruling governments and their ruling class. This fact is however conveniently ignored in favour of multiculturalism by pushing the agenda of diversity through strength in order to justify open borders.

The white Fathers of Confederation and their dream for Canada

The Fathers of Confederation are Canadian icons who are, more often than not, accredited with building Canada and making Canada what it is today. The Canada they are credited with building is a Canada that is inclusive and socially tolerant; it is the Canada we are presently familiar with and the Canada that politicians persistently boast about. But was it really possible for the Fathers of Confederation to actually envision a Canada as it actually is today? A Canada that has welcomed millions of immigrants and refugees; a Canada that has open its doors to ideologies

---

[131] https://twitter.com/CoryBMorgan/status/1194324794574946304

that defy the religious attributes aimed at creating and maintaining a colonial social structure; a Canada that has been instrumental in establishing a social phenomenon where colonialism is replaced with multiculturalism; a Canada which has no qualms about ignoring who the First Peoples are and how they have been forever displaced beyond the point of no return; a Canada that only offers mere lip service to Indigenous people as a recognition of tokenism by merely mentioning how this land is still theirs and how colonialism has wreaked havoc on them. You would be hard pressed to suggest that the dream of the Fathers of Confederation was to set aside the historical contributions of the Indigenous people and to place them into a token enclave of social distortion where they are repeatedly used as political pawns by every political establishment and politician in order to justify their own agenda. Unfortunately the dream of the Fathers of Confederation has been completely bastardized and replaced with a social experiment that makes colonialism look like a walk in the park. This social experiment is multiculturalism.

On July 1, 2014 Prime Minister Stephen Harper said that "In 1864, meeting in Charlottetown and in Quebec, our Fathers of Confederation dreamed a magnificent dream, a dream of a united Canada that would take its place among the countries of the world, prosperous, strong and free." "One hundred and forty-seven years later, this is their dream: Canada a confident partner, a courageous warrior, a compassionate neighbour. Canada, the best country in the world." [132] Indeed Canada is a great country and it's an even greater country for those political elites like Harper who are quick to spew some historical rhetoric that's more like a sound bite from a European history book issued to elementary school kids. This isn't an all out dump on Stephen Harper, but it's a mild example of how politicians forget to acknowledge that Canada is a country with a marred history regarding its Indigenous people. Harper was simply being a politician when he gave that speech and that's evident within the standard rhetoric he uses when describing Canada as a nation of a dream. Harper probably only repeated what his speech writers provided for him and it's a fine example of how politicians can get wrapped up in a political atmosphere that requires them to be considerate and culturally sensitive.

Social justice warriors are very quick to attack the colonials for occupying Indigenous lands, but yet they fully support open borders through the guise of multiculturalism. Multiculturalism, as the social justice warriors will argue, is a method of introducing different cultures that just happen to be non-white.

[132] https://www.theguardian.pe.ca/news/local/fathers-of-confederation-dreamed-a-magnificent-dream-harper-96718/

Remember, it was the white people who were the colonizers thus making them the original oppressors. So why then would it be acceptable for a white person, even if they were a social justice warrior, to endorse open borders under the guise of multiculturalism?

Well for politicians it's a simple way to appear to be considerate and culturally sensitive; as with the case of Stephen Harper. Stephen Harper is a perfect contemporary example of how the so-called right winged in Canada is nothing more than a group of politicians who exploit the harm that Canada's First Nation people have endured under white colonialism and how reconciliation should be achieved through social equality; mainly racial equality and how injecting massive amounts of non-white immigrants into Canadians society will somehow create a cultural utopia where past colonialism has been erased along with the damage colonialism did to the Indigenous people. Stephen Harper's speech easily demonstrates that there is no true *right-winged* facet inside Canada's political system whatsoever due to the fact that there is no objection to contemporary immigration, but instead there's a push for more immigration and a push for multiculturalism. When Stephen Harper was Prime Minister, his use of immigration and multiculturalism was just as much of a political tool as it was and is for the liberals, except for the constant use of how diversity will somehow be a source of strength thereby creating the cultural utopia where the harm caused by colonialism will utterly vanish into thin air. Hoping the colonial damage done to the Indigenous people will vanish into thin air, by promoting multiculturalism and acknowledging past colonialism, is once again demonstrated as being a tool utilized by the white person as a means of self-fulfilling virtue; and politicians know this best.

A settler is a settler is a settler just as a Canadian is a Canadian is a Canadian

Prime Minister Justin Trudeau infamously said that a Canadian is a Canadian is a Canadian[133] thus giving him a very special spot in contemporary history relating to the issue of citizenship. When Trudeau was expelling this disreputable quote, he inadvertently demeaned Canadian citizenship to something equivalent to a cheap cigar. Trudeau essentially established a precedent whereas anyone who comes to Canada with malevolent intentions, counter to what is expected in a civilized society, can always be considered a Canadian regardless of what crimes they commit; even if it's terrorism.[134] How can a concept like this even be remotely

---

[133] https://www.brainyquote.com/quotes/justin_trudeau_857562

acceptable in today's society and why aren't people screaming in protest at this utterly insane idea? The fact that Canada has been persistently described by politicians, intellectuals and mainstream media as an open, welcoming, tolerant and diverse country that was built off of immigration – and that any opposition to this is racism – would perhaps explain why there is no protest. Canadians have become socialized to the idea that Canada is a country built on immigration and that immigration is a necessary component to a functioning society regardless of how it still amounts to the contemporary colonization of Indigenous people and their lands.

Chapter 13: Multicultural and political Socialization.

> *Countries like Canada consistently have politicians and mainstream media promoting immigration at every turn and when anyone dares to question this multicultural socialization – such as a fringe media outlet – the accusations of racism, bigotry and xenophobia rapidly flow.*

Multicultural socialization is unique to white settler countries and is the main tool used to promote contemporary colonialism through multiculturalism. Countries like Canada consistently have politicians and the mainstream media promoting immigration at every turn and when anyone dares to question this multicultural socialization – such as a non-mainstream fringe media outlet – the accusations of racism, bigotry and xenophobia rapidly flow. Multicultural socialization begins when these accusations put the recipient in a position where they must defend themselves, thereby immediately distracting everyone away from the initial discussion in the first place. Indeed there have been people, the odd media outlet and politicians who opposed unfettered immigration and the concept that multiculturalism is supposed to be an integral element of Canadian society that should be embraced unquestionably, but they are swiftly painted as racist and anti-Canadian.

In contemporary Canadian society, where multiculturalism is enforced, there are absolutely no political parties whatsoever that are anti-immigration and barely no

---

[134] https://www.vice.com/en_us/article/7xaxby/a-canadian-is-a-canadian-liberal-leader-says-terrorists-should-keep-their-citizenship

politicians who oppose immigration. According to journalist Candice Malcom, current political parties don't oppose immigration they only oppose the abuse of immigration and its process. Malcom argues that this abuse of immigration demeans the value of being Canadian and that unfettered immigration does more harm than good when examined from an economic, safety and social standpoint.[135] Regardless of what journalists like Candice Malcom have to say or what politicians like Maxime Bernier have to say about unfettered immigration, they are still immediately labeled as racists therefore silencing the context of their arguments and concerns and forcing them into a false dichotomy. This is normal practice for politicians and the mainstream media and it's how the general public have become socialized into ignoring any disadvantages or problems associated with unfettered immigration and believing that multiculturalism is and always was the core identity of Canada. Support for unfettered immigration has become an expected theme of any political debate, ideology and agenda and the citizenry have been conditioned to expect it from politicians and if politicians don't mention it or oppose it then they're presumed and deemed as racist.

The development of political ideologies can be a very complex matter, but when it involves multiculturalism, political ideologies become simplified because multiculturalism is engrained into the Canadian culture through the long standing belief that Canada was built on immigration. Niemi and Hempurn 1995, suggest that political socialization begins at an early age and that this conditioning sets the stage for further reinforcement of a political ideology.[136] This can be witnessed in the positive support for multiculturalism and the many programs of immigration that allow hundreds of thousands of immigrants to settle in Canada each year. Mass media, schools and political events all play a pivotal role in developing a public attitude that multiculturalism and mass immigration is an essential part of the Canadian society and must be upheld at all cost. Mass media, schools and political events are also vital at reminding Canadians that they are on colonized lands and stolen from the Indigenous people and that reconciliation must be first and foremost in order to achieve a harmonious society.

Mass media – especially the CBC and other popular newspapers who receive government money for programming[137] [138] – all make headlines of stories that

---

[135] Losing True North: Justin Trudeau's Assault on Canadian Citizenship (2016)

[136] Niemi, Richard G., and Jane Junn. 1998. Civic Education: What Makes Students Learn? New Haven, CT: Yale University Press.

[137] https://www.cbc.ca/news/politics/journalism-support-fund-panel-1.5144282

[138] https://globalnews.ca/news/5328558/canada-media-fund/

involve how immigration is essential to sustain the Canadian way of life and how it has been a success and must continue at all cost. A key component to the positive aspect of large scale immigration that the mass media outlets report on is by linking mass immigration to multiculturalism, so that it can be perceived as being one, therefore clouding the distinction between the two. Mass immigration through family reunification, refugee intakes, record high numbers of permanent residency cards being awarded to foreign nationals and the many other generous immigration programs are all done under the guise that Canada is multicultural and mass immigration is a normal element of this multiculturalism. Mass media is pivotal in fusing the meanings of immigration and multiculturalism into a hybrid form that somehow means the same thing and creates a scenario where any opposition to multiculturalism is purely racist and anti-Canadian. At the same time, mass media is persistently reporting that the Indigenous people are the initial occupiers and owners of the land and resources and must always be respected as such and reconciliation is absolutely necessary. They also continually report on how colonialism has decimated their way of life and that reconciliation should be the primary agenda of politicians and any public policy relating to the use of natural resources and lands.

Schools ranging from grade school to post-secondary institutions all have immigration and multiculturalism incorporated into their curriculum as being a crucial part of Canadian society while also reinforcing the idea that its roots and structure are built from white colonialism.[139] Students are taught a variety of things that involve how the structure of Canada is multicultural in nature and that Canada is a country founded on immigration.[140] Students also learn that Canada has a horrible history in relation to the Indigenous people and that this horrible history is a direct result of white settler policies designed specifically to oppress the Indigenous people and to advance white ideology.[141] Schools infamously teach that it's this very white structure that is the foundation of all societal evils that oppress non-whites, while at the same time, encouraging mass immigration under the argument that Canada was founded by immigrants and it's only immigration that can make it better.[142] There are clearly conflicting values at place here, but this is the reality that all students will face when they are educated in Canada. Political

---

[139] http://www.cnmag.ca/kids-celebrating-diversity-in-our-schools/

[140] http://www.healthofchildren.com/M/Multicultural-Education-Curriculum.html

[141] http://behindthenumbers.ca/2015/02/25/teach-for-canada-de-or-re-colonizing-aboriginal-communities-in-canada/

[142] https://www.researchgate.net/publication/301746695_Diversity_and_Multicultural_Education_in_Canada

events are also another culprit of the false dichotomy between the necessity of mass immigration and the reconciliation with Indigenous people. Nearly every political event in Canada always includes the recognition of diversity as strength while acknowledging the need for reconciliation between the colonial establishment and the Indigenous people.

Mass media, schools and political events are complicit in creating an oxymoronic dilemma suggesting that lands stolen from the Indigenous people are an integral part of Canadian society and must be reconciled, while at the same time, continuing to ensure the very existence of a colonial structure by supporting continued immigration. Colonialism does not exist unless there is the occupation of lands, and this occupation requires immigration that allow non-Indigenous people to occupy Indigenous lands. Canadians, along with other colonized nations that practice multiculturalism, are in a direct conflict with the term *reconciliation* and *immigration* because of the competing dichotomy between the two ideologies. There can't be reconciliation for stolen lands while the lands are still being occupied for contemporary settlement by new immigrants. This competing dichotomy is not easily captured and critiqued by the average-everyday person yet alone by the academics, intellectuals, mainstream media or politicians. It is rather a concept that is completely missed despite being right in front of everyone's faces. Politically enforcing and socializing multiculturalism as an integral product of a country's blueprint, while espousing the notion of reconciliation, can only be possible when the two subject matters are kept separate from each other and are never integrated into one idea.

Mass media, schools and political events never mention the two subjects collectively, but do constantly make mention of the subjects individually at different times according to the context they are needed. Journalist Brian Lilly questioned this competing dichotomy when he outlined how a university professor advocated the intake of large numbers of middle eastern refugees while also claiming that the *canoe* is a symbol of oppression and colonialism and that merely saying that you're Canadian means that you're part of the oppressive colonial establishment.[143] Linking the two concepts of this competing dichotomy would amount to an acknowledgement of failure thus placing the entire arguments into ill repute and disenfranchising the foundation of the argument proving it as oxymoronic. Political socialization is the reason why people don't rise up and

---

[143] https://youtu.be/u-ixXleiA8s

demand that colonialism, disguised as programs of mass immigration such as multiculturalism, should cease and desist. This political socialization from the mass media, schools and political events[144] is the reason the settlement of millions of new people in Canada is celebrated as an achievement and the reason why opposition to this contemporary settlement is deemed as racist. Society is moulded into believing that past and present immigration is the key aspect that is a unifying national element that must be preserved. When critiquing the notion that immigration is a unifying national element it can be easy to assume that it's the concept of a left winged political facet – which is generally true – but all too often conservatives can hold the supposition that a country was founded off of immigration and that immigration can be an underlining principle of that country's heritage therefore unifying it nationally. Conservative writer Matt Walsh of The Young America's Foundation alludes to this when he describes immigration as a unifying foundational *thing* whereas he believes that race, skin colour or ethnicity was never the unifying principle in America and that being so was, and is, what separates America from every other country thus creating a doctrine of human rights.[145] Essentially Walsh strongly suggest that it is the diversity through immigration that unifies America creating an equitable society that is a true example of how human rights are paramount. The idea of a unifying national *thing* through immigration demonstrates how political socialization makes it perfectly acceptable to justify multiculturalism as a normal function of contemporary society, despite the fact that contemporary society was formed on stolen land by using immigration to do so.

The post-colonial concept of multiculturalism versus immigration – and how it's politically socialized upon us

> *You can't have colonialism without immigration and you can't have multiculturalism without immigration so the two terms are unified as a key element of past and present colonialism.*

Multiculturalism and immigration are two terms that are synonymously used when most people give any thought to the national diversity, immigration programs and

---

[144] https://www.oxfordhandbooks.com/view/10.1093/oxfordhb/9780199935307.001.0001/oxfordhb-9780199935307-e-98

[145] https://youtu.be/xQQEWGUTCwl

Canadian citizenship. They are however different in their actual meaning: immigration is the travel to another country for the purposes of obtaining permanent citizenship,[146] and multiculturalism is the presence of, or support for the presence of, several distinct cultural or ethnic groups within a society.[147] Where the two terms begin to morph into one is when they are examined from the perspective of how colonialism was and is still being carried out. The two terms have become contemporarily unified as the debate between national identity and diversity takes hold. It can easily be said that multiculturalism is simply a bundle of immigration policies that allow for a racially diverse group of non-Indigenous people to become citizens and settle on lands that once belonged to the Indigenous people. A major component of colonialism was the importation of non-Indigenous people to support the colonial establishment and to build and support the colonial society; and these non-Indigenous people were white. You can't have colonialism without immigration and you can't have multiculturalism without immigration so the two terms are unified as a key element of past and present colonialism. The key aspect of multiculturalism however is that the people being imported are not the usual representation of a white colonial structure, but are instead ethnically diverse. This allows the white structure to have a means of distracting people away from the oppressive nature of colonialism while allowing them to maintain colonial control by the use of its major component: that major component being immigration. Colonial powers can still implement the importation of people to the occupied lands and then demand that even further land and resources are needed to facilitate the settlement of the newly arrived people.

The difference is that the people being imported to sustain contemporary colonialism aren't white because multiculturalism is not conducive with the importation of white people due to the correlation between whiteness and colonialism. Multiculturalism is an ideology perpetrated by white folks in order to ensure that a status quo of immigration is maintained thereby allowing for continued colonization in a contemporary form that will require the occupation of more land. Despite multiculturalism being defined as the celebration of different cultures, multiculturalism can't even exist without the generous immigration policies that current governments endorse and hold to the highest admiration. These policies of immigration are the many programs that allow large numbers of non-Indigenous/non-white people to immigrate to an already colonized land.

---

[146] https://www.merriam-webster.com/dictionary/immigration
[147] https://www.merriam-webster.com/dictionary/multiculturalism

Programs such as the temporary foreign worker program, family reunification, government and private sponsored refugee programs, skilled and professional workers intakes, unskilled worker programs and the regular programs of immigration that are streamlined in order for governments to meet their high target numbers.

It's a proficient way for the white establishment to covertly maintain and gain more power and encroach further on the Indigenous people and their lands. Immigration and multiculturalism are therefore two terms that can be used interchangeably due to the fact that they both are a celebrated product of white colonialism. Using immigration and multiculturalism interchangeably is a distraction used by the the white establishment to convince people that colonialism is actually an equitable way of achieving liberty, freedom and prosperity for all. This form of contemporary colonialism is simply referred to as multiculturalism and is a strong social component that endorses mass immigration while encouraging everyone to celebrate diversity as strength. Diversity then becomes the calling card for social change in order to ameliorate the past injustices of white colonialism and then is exploited by politicians for the purpose of gaining and maintaining power while further being used to silence critics by labeling them as racist. Multiculturalism is therefore multifaceted in its execution whereas it involves large scale immigration, the implementation of ethnic diversity and the requirement of unquestionable loyalty from everyone.

A post-colonial society is one that represents diversity as strength and mass immigration through multiculturalism

Colonized white settler countries use many programs and methods of immigration so that they can maintain their colonial status quo allowing them to continue increasing the population thus creating a further demand for land, resources and services. As long as the politicians keep proclaiming that immigration policies are to maintain a certain status quo or be increased, multiculturalism serves as a means to ensure that society is open and inclusive – just the same as past colonialism – while producing an environment that prohibits questioning or challenging the status quo: unless you want accusations of racism thrown at you. Instead the idea of *post-colonialism* is touted as a solution to remedy the past injustices. Post colonialism in contemporary Canadian society is a dashing idea that suggests that the old white colonial ways are a thing of the past and that Canada can move forward despite all of its unscrupulous white history. This white history is one that has been a historical blemish consisting of residential schools, stealing Indigenous land, forced sterilization of Indigenous people, removing Indigenous children from their homes, dishonouring treaties and numerous other forms of institutional and systemic discrimination and oppression. The biggest aspect of past white colonialism was the systemic promotion of mass immigration of non-Indigenous settlers who were needed to occupy the empty lands and to develop the resources through farming and developing these lands. The post-colonial Canada of today however has absolutely no intention of doing any such thing as occupy more land or to develop any resources; at least on the forefront. Post-colonialism in today's Canada is only about reconciliation and acknowledging the wrongs of the past and promising to never do harm again. Post-colonialism can brazenly suggest that there's no longer a king or queen who represents a white monarchy that is forcing the immigration of alike people onto the Indigenous people and their lands. Post colonialism should however suggest that there will be no further immigration into Indigenous lands and that all remnants of whiteness has left the country completely never to return, therefore allowing Indigenous people to self govern as they wish. Fundamentally, post-colonialism should be the complete decolonization of all white European ideologies and all whiteness within the once colonized society. The entire eradication of white European ideologies and whiteness is something of an understatement: it's highly unlikely that people of European descent would ever pick up and leave returning to their ancestral lands. If so, this would mean that the vast majority of politicians themselves would have to join the queue at the airport with the other vast majority of Canadians who are also white. Decolonization would also mean that the entire political system and economic structure would have to be completely dismantled and rebuilt so that it doesn't represent whiteness and European colonialism.

Therefore, the term *post-colonialism* would require a one hundred percent complete makeover of the entire nation and virtually every aspect of the nation's identity would need to be erased. Most of all, this would mean that all immigration in its entirety would need to cease immediately and not be reinstated. The magnitude of this sort of purge would render this an impossibility by today's standards because nobody who is non-Indigenous is leaving the country for the sake of reconciliation. On top of this, terminating immigration would actually destroy the foundation of contemporary colonialism for what it is: contemporary colonialism being a reincarnation of European whiteness and all the privileges that it entails due to the fact that it is a white man's philosophy that is cleverly disguised with the intention of overwhelming the nation with the importation of non-Indigenous people. This clever disguise of European colonialism is called multiculturalism and it's goal is to bring about a utopia of social harmony that politicians call *diversity through strength*. Multiculturalism is meant to bring in large numbers of contemporary non-Indigenous settlers who will require the resources of the country such as land, natural resources, social programs and many other instituted platforms that are said will enhance the lives of Canadians and make Canada the envy of the world. And of course we are again reminded that Canada is a country that was built by immigration so if you oppose this concept you're racist. A post-colonial society is nothing different than the colonial society of the past: the immigration of non-Indigenous people who occupy Indigenous lands then develop the resources to build a country.

Post-colonialism is a buzzword for/defining reconciliation

Defining post-colonialism in its raw form clearly indicates that it has very little to do with the actual decolonization of occupying white European forces. Instead, post-colonialism has become a buzzword for politicians, academics and social justice warriors who claim that contemporary society is more or less a theatre for the study of how colonialism created hardships for the Indigenous people. To argue that we live in post-colonial times might therefore be an accurate statement if it is viewed through that school of thought. It can therefore appear that we live in a post-colonial era allowing people to sit back and critique how the white colonial powers have damaged and completely destroyed the Indigenous people while demanding that the institutions of white colonialism end immediately. While this critiquing is being done, there's never any suggestion of actual decolonization, only the position that contemporary society is responsible for the past injustices committed against the Indigenous people. Those folks insisting that we are in post colonial times, and who offer so much unsolicited opinions as to how bad contemporary society is in terms of social and racial inequities, never suggest how to solve the initial *problem* that they claim to be fighting: the *problem* of how whiteness has decimated the Indigenous people and how it acts to keep them continually oppressed. Truly solving the problem of white European occupation would involve the complete removal of the entire white European establishment and returning the lands back to the Indigenous people. Doing this would be actual decolonization and it is a far stretch from claiming that contemporary society is post-colonial by critiquing every imperceptible aspect of it.

What we constantly hear from the politicians, intellectuals, social justice warriors – and especially white ones – is that there must be full reconciliation with the Indigenous people and that reconciliation must be the paramount aspect in a post-colonial society. Simply put, post-colonialism is only a word that is used to make the person advocating for equality sound virtuous and give credit to their standing as a social justice advocate. In order to have a genuine post-colonial society there must be complete decolonization, and decolonization must involved the entire removal of all whiteness in society that relates to the initial European occupation, especially the removal of all non-Indigenous people. As radical as that sounds it's clearly the only true way a *post-colonial* society could and would exist. The radicalness of this ideology is something that would only come about by way of a revolution that would redefine society in such a way as to erase all colonial elements and then restructure it to reflect Indigenous people's values, culture and their original way of life.

Using post-colonial elements of critical race theory, suggesting the entire social, cultural, political and legal systems must be demolished from the top-down then rebuilt from the bottom up, is what a revolution would look like.[148] Even if a revolution used the play books of post-colonial critical race theory, it's very unlikely that Canada, or any other white settler society, would ever undertake measures of this magnitude. But talk of such revolutionary prospects would surely hoist the excitement of those academics, intellectuals and social justice warriors who would foam at the mouth thinking about such a revolt. Instead, those foamy mouths advocates demand reconciliation as their revolution, while at the same time, screaming for open borders and mass immigration, thereby devaluing the term *post-colonialism.* The term, decolonization, has been cleverly replaced with the word *reconciliation,* and this word is what encourages social justice advocates to think that the term post-colonialism actually has integrity of some sort. Post-colonialism is a bunkum term that sounds as if though it has some clout and can be a solution to the problem of white European colonialism and all the troubles it has caused for the Indigenous people. Post-colonialism has absolutely nothing to do with decolonization or returning the lands and resources to the Indigenous people; as it should according to its raw face value definition. The term post-colonialism is synonymous with the term reconciliation and the two can often be used interchangeably as a means of showing some kind of noble social advocacy towards Indigenous people.

---

[148] https://digitalcommons.law.villanova.edu/cgi/viewcontent.cgi?article=3102&context=vlr

Reconciliation is the main term used as a solution in contemporary society that acknowledges the wrongs that white European colonialism has brought upon the Indigenous people. Recognizing these wrongs is what a post-colonial society is, but simply recognizing the wrongs and offering apologies is not going to rectify the past. Post-colonialism has absolutely nothing to do with true reconciliation; especially when the same people who advocate reconciliation only do so by merely acknowledging that we live in post-colonial times, and then at the same time, advocate for multiculturalism and all its glory. Examples of what a post-colonial society is can be witnessed when there are demands for apologies, demands for amelioration, demands for recognition of victim status and demands for compensation. When colonial forces adhere to these demands as an act of penance, it can now be virtuously named *reconciliation,* and then it can be stated that we now live in a post-colonial era despite the ongoing issue where the residual cohorts of white colonialism still remain: especially the residual cohorts through the continued mass immigration of non-Indigenous people.

Multiculturalism in lieu of decolonization then renamed as post-colonialism

A post-colonial society in Canada is one that embraces multiculturalism and diversity while proclaiming that this diversity – this non-Indigenous diversity – is a source of social strength. This embracement of diversity is what politicians, academics, open border advocates, intellectuals and social justice warriors claim is a source of social strength and social cohesion and is what makes Canada a great country. Multiculturalism is how a post-colonial society is defined and this definition is reflected by the support of those people who champion all forms of unfettered immigration as a source of national strength. The province of Manitoba proudly promotes government mandated cultural diversity through the Manitoba Multiculturalism Act where they take pride in being multicultural and where they further promote diversity as a fundamental characteristic that benefits all Manitobans.[149] This celebration of diversity is possibly fuelled by the damage that white European colonialism inflicted on the Indigenous people of Manitoba inciting the advocacy of the social justice warriors to remedy it. The social justice warriors all have the same traits where they advocate mass immigration while they fully respect and acknowledge the plight of the Indigenous people. When the government implements an obligation to celebrate multiculturalism and Indigenous culture together, we can clearly witness contradictions between the two schools of

---

[149] https://www.gov.mb.ca/chc/multiculturalism/index.html

thought. This contradiction was demonstrated when the Canadian national anthem was sung in the Indigenous people's language of Ojibwa during a Winnipeg Jets game[150] therefore demonstrating a noble act of cultural recognition and social solidarity, all while being sung in a city that is solemnly multicultural and celebrates it accordingly. Despite the prevalent contradictions that make the entire concept of multiculturalism nothing more than a political *feel-good* stunt, there are still plenty of intellectuals ready to remind us how bad colonialism is.

Mary Jane Logan McCallum, Adele Perry[151] and Heather Dorries, et al.[152], have published extensive written works that clearly outline how colonialism, past and present, have had extremely negative consequences for the Indigenous people in Canada. So it's clear in this case that there are competing dichotomies relating to Indigenous people, colonialism and multiculturalism: three competing dichotomies in fact. The first is how Manitoba proclaims to be an open and diverse society, through multiculturalism where they celebrate immigration so that everyone can supposedly live harmoniously. Second is that the Indigenous people are recognized and bestowed the right to display their traditional language within the national anthem at a sporting event. Third is the respected and learned intellectuals who have extensively studied and articulately identified the past and present damage that white European colonialism has caused the Indigenous people through the institutionalized and systemic white structures. Using cultural diversity as a means to eliminate racism has become a spin-off of multiculturalism and the means to promote a racially equal society. Governments, social justice advocates, intellectuals, academics and the majority of Canadians all believe that multiculturalism is what defines Canada as a prosperous and socially equitable nation. It's this concept of multiculturalism that is consistent with the school of thought that Canada is a nation built off of immigration and it is this immigration that makes Canada a great country. This same school of thought will also insist that immigration is continually needed in order to maintain a successful nation and that multiculturalism is the key to ensure further success during contemporary times.

---

[150] https://winnipeg.ctvnews.ca/national-anthem-sung-in-ojibwa-at-winnipeg-jets-game-1.4773195
[151] Structures of Indifference: An Indigenous Life and Death in a Canadian City
Mary Jane Logan McCallum (Author), Adele Perry (Author)
Published September 2018, 144 pages
Paper, ISBN: 978-0-88755-835-1
[152] Settler City Limits: Indigenous Resurgence and Colonial Violence in the Urban Prairie West
Heather Dorries (Editor), Robert Henry (Editor), David Hugill (Editor), Tyler McCreary (Editor), Julie Tomiak (Editor)
Published October 2019, 368 pages
Paper, ISBN: 978-0-88755-843-6

Oddly enough, the same aforementioned people who adhere to the concept that immigration is necessary also avow that Canada has a major problem with racism: racism that is a direct result of the whiteness that colonialism has established. The government nevertheless has a solution to the ill effects of colonialism and the racism it has created through the past policies that enforced whiteness by declaring the necessity of a post-colonial society that is ethnically diverse and multiculturalism is the way to achieve this.

The idea of post-colonialism is however strapped against the notion of diversity – the diversity of non-Indigenous people – and the notion that Indigenous people themselves are to be acknowledged as the true possessors of the lands and resources. This post-colonial idea is something that makes the white person feel good and feel virtuous essentially vindicating them as an oppressor of sorts. It also allows the white person to justify further colonization of Indigenous lands and resources by using the element of multiculturalism that can only be successful by using immigration. Politicians will sidestep the fact that immigration is a key component of multiculturalism, just as it was with colonialism, by referring to the need to build a new relationship with the Indigenous people. This new relationship would involve rewriting damaging policies of the past and acknowledging once again that the Indigenous people were and are stakeholders in the development and maintaining Canadian society through legislation and policies that involve mandatory consultation with them on issues potentially impacting them.[153] Multiculturalism is one issue that is not on the government's agenda with relation to any mandatory consultations, but multiculturalism is still being used as a key component to substantially increase the population in white settler Canada in order to justify the need to expropriate more land and resources.

Chapter 14: Canada: the greatest yet racist country in the world that everyone wants to come to.

> *The people who support mass immigration, the government who mandates official multiculturalism and those who earnestly believe that Canada belongs to the Indigenous people are also the ones who also fervently claim that Canada is painfully racist.*

---

[153] https://pm.gc.ca/en/news/news-releases/2018/02/14/government-canada-create-recognition-and-implementation-rights

If Canadian society is one that reeks so badly of racism due to past colonialism and the whiteness it created then why do so many people from all over the world want to immigrate here and settle? The answer to this question may not be as easy to answer as it might seem. The people who support mass immigration, the government who mandates official multiculturalism and those who earnestly believe that Canada belongs to the Indigenous people are also the ones who fervently claim that Canada is painfully racist. This sentiment of how racist Canada is, despite being multicultural, is actually very prevalent and is the basis for the argument that more needs to be done to correct the racist structure. Charles Officer believes that Canada is a beacon of diversity and has given so many immigrants of colour a wonderful opportunity for a better life. Unfortunately Officer also holds a strong postulation that Canada is inherently racist due to systemic racism embedded within the social fabric. This embedded racism that Officer eludes to is largely based on his personal experiences growing up in Toronto where he was racially profiled by the police and where he experienced racial discrimination while playing hockey. The unfortunate experiences Officer endured inspired him to make a film where he highlights racial inequalities within a multicultural society and how being a multicultural society doesn't necessarily set a standard for automatic racial equality.[154]

It sounds rather illogical that racism is so prevalent in a multicultural society like Canada and that this racism is having adverse effects on people of colour; especially considering how governments have made diversity a main social objective and a major part of their political platforms. But nevertheless, there are social activists who cite evidence that multicultural Canada has so much racism in it that Canadians aren't even aware that it exists. A survey by the Environics Institute for Survey Research and the Canadian Race Relations Foundation indicated that the majority of Canadians feel that race relations are generally good in Canada, but that reports of racism are on the rise.[155] Social activist Desmond Cole believes that Canadians are overlooking the prevalence of systemic racism by mistaking it for individual acts of racism and not part of a larger socially ingrained issue. Cole states that many Canadians are aware that racism is an issue, but these same people oppose any government intervention into addressing the issue.[156]

---

[154] https://www.cbc.ca/firsthand/m_blog/dont-believe-the-hype-canada-is-not-a-nation-of-cultural-tolerance
[155] https://www.environicsinstitute.org/projects/project-details/race-relations-in-canada-2019
[156] https://www.ctvnews.ca/canada/racism-not-a-big-problem-activist-says-survey-shows-canadians-in-denial-

Essentially, Canadians can fully acknowledge the prevalence of racism but are too scared to tackle it. This certainly conflicts with the notion that Canada is a country built by immigration and that further immigration is needed in order to sustain the national identity and economy. After all, politicians are constantly pushing the narrative of strength through diversity and that achieving this strength is reflected in multiculturalism as a core national identity. So it would only be prudent for the vast majority of Canadians to hold the viewpoint that racism is not a serious issue and that most folks live in relative harmony due to multiculturalism. Activists like Cole can always critique things from a personal standpoint where they have experienced acts of racism themselves despite living in a multicultural city and country. It should always go without saying that there is never any excuse for racism, especially in a multicultural country that prides itself on immigration as a core quality that built the country in the first place.

What the analysis of activists like Cole and Officer provide us is an insight into a further problem of potential hypocrisy within a system that is built on racial diversity, but somehow fails to be racially equal on a social level. Governments at all levels demand the immigration of people from non-white countries and throw their political and bureaucratic weight behind the concept that Canada is a multicultural country that was exclusively built on immigration. This would mean that it is essential for Canada to acquire as many immigrants as possible in order to ensure continued success as a racially diverse nation and to ensure even greater success in the future. It therefore stands to reason that governments at all levels are proclaiming that Canada is a country that is specifically designed for racial diversity and that issues of racism are negligible at best. After all, diversity is believed to be a Canadian emblem of social strength so why would there be racism and why would so many non-whites give near anything to be a Canadian citizen?

There are many reasons why Canada is an extremely attractive country for people to immigrate to, but mainly it's the individual freedoms that are offered and the fact that Canada is touted as a multicultural nation. Many immigrants who seek Canada as a place to settle feel welcomed due to the open immigration process that is relatively simple and straightforward. The economy, a fair and inclusive political system, numerous employment opportunities, universal public health care, numerous social programs offering a social safety net and a world class education system also add to the reasons why people want to settle in Canada.[157] On top of

---

1.4724713

[157] https://www.randstad.ca/job-seeker/career-resources/working-in-canada/11-reasons-canadas-an-awesome-

these reasons for contemporary immigrants wanting to settle in Canada is the fact that the government will capitalize on a political opportunity to endorse Canada's multicultural identity by virtually opening the borders to anyone who claims some type of asylum or refugee status. This is currently being witnessed at the Quebec and the United States border where tens of thousands of people literally walked into Canada claiming asylum over fears of being deported out of the U.S. The federal government of Canada put in place immediate measures to welcome the illegal border crossers and set them up with housing, health care and a path to citizenship. Even if the illegal border crossers didn't immediately report to the proper legal authorities upon their entry, municipalities would offer sanctuary to them so that they could avoid legal prosecution or deportation. This upstanding act of protecting illegal immigrants who want to settle in Canada demonstrates how political capital can be gained by showing that diversity and inclusiveness is a key feature of the *Canadian way*.

Politicians jump on this opportunity and advertise that they will offer illegal crossers a chance at gaining a taste of Canadian inclusiveness and equality. This inclusiveness and equality is what is being sold as the *Canadian way* and politicians at the municipal level offer this by claiming that their jurisdiction is a *sanctuary* for illegal immigrants. The term sanctuary cities are synonymous with the harbouring of illegal immigrants who either fail to report to authorities upon entry or who have overstayed their temporary visas. Politicians within these sanctuary cities will often instruct their police departments not to enforce any federal immigration rules and not to report any immigration violations to the federal authorities. This sounds like an honourable thing to do for the people who are seeking a better life and who are fleeing persecution and it also sounds like an attempt to advertise racial diversity as a form of social strength. It would therefore blatantly suggest that the sanctuary city is one that is racially equal and that racism is a moot issue due to its apparent strength through diversity and racism essentially shouldn't exist. This however may not be the case as many illegal immigrants face racism within these sanctuary cities. The racism they face comes by way of local authorities not adhering to the measures of a sanctuary city when they report an illegal immigrant to the federal authorities or when they act on behalf of federal authorities. This could be a interpreted as an example of systemic racism and a failure of adhering to multiculturalism, especially when politicians announce that they support sanctuary cities because diversity is their strength.[158] Above and

---

beyond any systemic issues of racism in Canada there is still the issue of individual racism that threatens the multicultural aspirations.

With multiculturalism comes the automatic need for the mass immigration of many different people in order to build a society that is representative of a racially diverse nation so that politicians can honour themselves as social victors. Simply because Canada opens its borders to massive amounts of new settlers doesn't necessarily mean that they won't face some form of racism: in fact there's actually a high probability of contemporary settlers facing racial discrimination. The Ryerson Centre for Immigration and Settlement suggest that new immigrants face a high probability of experiencing racism in Canada despite it being an open, welcoming and multicultural country.[159] The racial discrimination that new settlers can experience are both systemic and individual and can result in a conflict between the ideology of diversity as a form of strength. When this happens, the entire concept of multiculturalism becomes problematic due to the fact that Canada is presumed to be a great nation that was founded and built by immigrant settlers. Despite the fact that Canada is constantly flaunted as a country of immigrants, many people from contemporary generations will contend that Canada is nevertheless a nation stolen from the Indigenous people. This is because academia often uses post-modernist versions of history where white students are made to feel that it was their ancestors that stole the land from the Indigenous people [160] therefore placing the onus on them to rectify the wrongs of the past by insinuating that they created a racist society. This concept is what encourages whites to become social justice advocates for the Indigenous people and people of colour and to endorse open immigration policies.

Racial discrimination of this nature highlights how there is a strong degree of ignorance within a so-called diverse society that promotes values of multiculturalism. It also raises the question as to how racism can even exist in such a society and why do so many people want to settle here despite the overt racism plaguing society? The answer may be somewhat complex requiring a deep analysis into how social behaviour can allow for such a contradiction to prevail. Nevertheless, there is a clear contradiction relating to the high levels of racism that Canada is said to have and the demand for citizenship from people who believe

---

[158] https://rabble.ca/news/2017-03-01t000000/dont-be-fooled-sanctuary-city-trend-migrants-canada-are-still-risk
[159] https://digital.library.ryerson.ca/islandora/object/RULA%3A8432/datastream/OBJ/download/Discrimination_experienced_by_landed_immigrants_in_Canada_.pdf
[160] Canada in Decay:Mass Immigration, Diversity, and the Ethnocide of Euro-Canadians. (2008) P.69

that Canada is perhaps the greatest country in the world. The contradiction between the high levels of racism and the demand to gain citizenship –despite the high racism, may be do to the fact that all levels of government sell Canada as a multicultural nation that was founded and built by immigration and that this immigration must continue in order to keep Canada great therefore suggesting that Canada needs immigrants. The idea that making, and keeping, Canada great through the process of immigration is a concept that is widely supported by Will Kymlicka who holds that Western nations must be open to immigration and ethnic diversity. Kymlicka believes that immigration won't damage the fabric of a Western society so long as the governmental policies ensure that the immigration is one that is necessary, such as skilled labourers for example.[161] For this reason Kymlicka and many others support and justify the concept of mass immigration under the program of multiculturalism without any thought being given to how colonial immigration was also a program that endorsed mass immigration in order to have skilled and unskilled workers who are constantly credited with building the foundation of contemporary society. Although you will never hear the likes of Kymlicka or his cohorts ever draw a comparison between early colonial immigration and contemporary immigration as something that is similar in nature, you will definitely hear them spew the repeated statements that Canada is a country that was built by immigrants while forgetting that it was also the exact same racist colonial policies that they say utterly destroyed the Indigenous people and stole their land. It would seem what Kymlicka is essentially suggesting is that for a settler to go back to their ancestral land would be like an Indigenous person going back to their old ways; so what can be done now? All the modern technology enjoyed today is from colonialism and you could make the argument that for better or worse the Indigenous people are where they are on a socially-technological level because of colonialism. But to make an argument like this in what is proclaimed to be a post-colonial society would surely be viewed as racist and immediately shut down. In fact there would be no viable defence to the accusation of racism, even if you could objectively propose that it was colonialism that placed everyone in the contemporary position they are in now: especially when including the concept of multiculturalism. Overcoming an accusation of racism – after suggesting that it was colonialism itself that put us all here, would be the best approach to convey the point that contemporary immigration policies are far worse than those colonial ones from the past. The unfortunate irony is that contemporary academic thinkers

---

[161] Kymlicka, Will. (2003) 195-208. Immigration, Citizenship, Multiculturalism

like Kymlicka aren't capable of stepping out of their comfort zone of the *oppressor verses the oppressed* due to the popularity within mainstream academia relating to this concept; and not to mention how socialized today's society is to the political concept of strength through diversity.

Chapter 15 where do we go from here?

Where do we go from here is an excellent question that is unlikely to be answered too diligently. As I've already mentioned in this book, post-colonialism in its true definition should entail the entire removal of all colonial reminisce to such an extent that all non-Indigenous people be expelled and the land and resources in it's entirety be returned to its rightful owners: the Indigenous people. It is obvious that those who speak of the damage that colonialism has caused the Indigenous people are also the ones who speak of how wonderfully amazing Canada is in terms of multiculturalism and the diversity it creates and how immigration built the country. This has created fertile ground where there are no qualms whatsoever about uniting a social cause of racial inequality between two or more intersecting groups that attach themselves to the plight of the Indigenous people. It has become rather socially fashionable for groups of non-Indigenous people to find common grounds of some kind of oppression that stems from colonialism. This has been a popular theme for the Black Lives Matter movement that is sweeping North America where they seek common ground with Indigenous people then demand that all people proclaim that black lives matter and if you question this proclamation you're racist. The intersecting of these social causes has become so fashionable that even the LGTBQ2+ groups have found common ground with the Indigenous people where they too claim to be victims of oppression due to colonialism. Yes of course black lives absolutely matter and there is no doubt that black people in Canada have suffered racism, discrimination and bigotry that can be contributed to colonialism. The argument that is made by the BLM folks is that Canada, as a white settler society, has been systematically and institutionally racist toward people of colour due to the structure of whiteness within society. This concept allows an open door for social justice warriors to capitalize on virtue and lobby politicians for recognition and change. The issue is however that change is something that has already happened do to the social and political nature of contemporary society that has erased all antiquated laws and policies that purposely oppressed non-white people. Currently in today's society, there are no laws, policies or regulations on the books that would institutionally discriminate against any person of colour or target them for systemic oppression of any sorts. In fact, Canada is the most progressive country in the world regarding racial equality and the elimination of racism both institutionally and systemically. Where we go from here can be answered in the following simple question: if Canada is so blatantly racist and oppressive towards non-white people then why isn't there a mass exodus of people wanting to leave Canada? That question will never be answered because even those people who absolutely detest Canada will never leave and those who aren't even in Canada want nothing more then to come to Canada and become citizens. This book has repeatedly reiterated the fact that Canada is a white settler country that was built on the immigration of white colonial powers that established a system of whiteness and those powers of whiteness did oppress the Indigenous people thus changing the course of their lives forever. This book also reiterates the fact that Canada is proudly touted as a country of immigrants and it was this immigration that built the contemporary success of the country. This book also reiterates how multiculturalism is simply another process of mass immigration of non-Indigenous people and how they are being praised as tokens of contemporary racial equality by politicians, academics and social justice warriors. These very same supporters of multiculturalism are also the very ones who constantly remind everyone how racist and horrible Canada is due to its white settler heritage and all the whiteness it produces stemming from colonialism. What there is now in Canada is multiculturalism and that is what post colonialism is called in a white settler society. Colonialism has been replaced with multiculturalism and multiculturalism is the contemporary version of colonialism plain and simple. The best we're going to see in terms of any kind of actual post colonialism is just the continued mass immigration of non-Indigenous people – as it was centuries ago – and continued political rhetoric stating that Canada needs immigrants and that Canada owes the Indigenous people reconciliation due to colonialism. Multiculturalism is the bloodless revolution that will only cause further harm to the Indigenous people who will be pushed to the back burner of society. By failing to recognize how harmful immigration can be for the Indigenous people then take some time to consider how immigration literally wiped out the Beothuk people of Newfoundland.

A post-colonial society should be one that fully recognizes the Indigenous people as the founding peoples who have a fundamental right to self governance and an entitlement to reconciliation for the injustices that colonialism placed upon them. These words are very powerful and politically charged. These words are part of a common theme that politicians spewed regularly for decades to no actual avail. We also hear politicians constantly spew how diversity is our strength and that immigration is needed now more than ever.

Conclusion

Contemporary society is so entrenched with the idea that Canada can't be a country without immigration and lots of it at that, which begs the question, did the early immigrants who are credited with building the country steal the land from the Indigenous people and how can further immigration be justified as a good thing? Every current politician, intellectual and nearly every citizen would all agree that immigration is an absolute must in order to sustain and advance society. Despite the fact that the correlation between immigration and colonialism is right in front of our faces, it's extremely difficult to see due to the idea that Canada is touted as a country of immigrants and somehow diversity is an essential and necessary trait that forms the national foundation and identity. We are then promptly reminded of how white European colonialism has utterly destroyed the Indigenous people by robbing them of their lands and resources and then subjecting them to white colonial rule thus permanently marginalizing them. Furthermore, we are compelled by government mandate to celebrate multiculturalism as a national unifying element in defiance of the fact that multiculturalism is just a covert method of mass immigration. The covert method of immigration is simply a contemporary form of colonialism where more non-Indigenous people are injected into the colonized lands therefore securing a greater foothold of government control over the stolen lands and ensuring that Canada will always and forever be a country of immigrants who destroyed the Indigenous people.

Multiculturalism has become the modern means that politicians use to rationalize the appropriation of lands and resources while superficially forgiving themselves of past colonialism that laid out the ground-work for contemporary colonialism called multiculturalism. Through multiculturalism, white colonialism continues and the Indigenous people will be further subjected to the covert power of whiteness and all its propagating destructive glory that is disguised through the frivolous concept of strength through diversity and how Canada is a country of immigrants.

Postscript:

It had been an enduring honour and pleasure to write this book over the last three years in average increments of 20 minutes a day. Yes I am aware that there are many repetitive phrases and a constant bombardment of the main concept. I used this literary approach out of lack of experience in writing books as it's the only feasible means I could find to hammer out the theoretical point of how contemporary immigration is no better than past immigration: in fact it's substantially worse. The truly sad thing is that nearly every person in the country is completely blind to the correlation between how multiculturalism is merely a modern form of past colonialism plain and simple. 2020 was certainly a very strange year so I figured it best to ensure that if one thing I would remember 2020 for is that I finished and published my first book.

www.ingramcontent.com/pod-product-compliance
Lightning Source LLC
Chambersburg PA
CBHW081517250726
48659CB00009B/2844